Trading Rules that Work

Trading Rules that Work

The 28 Essential Lessons Every Trader Must Master

JASON ALAN JANKOVSKY

John Wiley & Sons, Inc.

Published by John Wiley & Sons, Inc., Hoboken, New Jersey.
Published simultaneously in Canada.

For general information on our other products and services or for technical support, please contact our Customer Care Department within the United States at (800) 762-2974, outside the United States at (317) 572-3993 or fax (317) 572-4002.

Wiley also publishes its books in a variety of electronic formats. Some content that appears in print may not be available in electronic books. For more information about Wiley products, visit our web site at www.wiley.com.

Library of Congress Cataloging-in-Publication Data:

Jankovsky, Jason Alan, 1961–
    Trading rules that work : the 28 essential lessons every trader must master / Jason Alan Jankovsky.
      p. cm. — (Wiley trading series)
    Includes bibliographical references and index.
    ISBN-13 978-0-471-79216-1 (cloth)
    ISBN-10 0-471-79216-0 (cloth)
    1. Speculation. 2. Investment analysis. 3. Futures. 4. Foreign exchange.
  I. Title. I. Series.
  HG6015.J36 2007
  332.64—dc22

                                          2006014076

Printed in the United States of America.

10 9 8 7 6 5 4 3 2 1

The fault, dear Brutus, is not in our stars,
but in ourselves, that we are underlings.
—William Shakespeare

Contents

Acknowledgments

Special thanks to those helped me stay focused on completing this manuscript on time: my editor, Kevin Cummins, who just let me work but reminded me that deadlines are part of the business; Emilie Herman at Wiley for being so patient with my lack of computer skills and endless questions; the staff at Infinity Brokerage and ProEdgeFX, who allowed me to work after hours with company equipment to finish the manuscript; Jim Cagnina and Jim Mooney at Infinity, who encouraged Wiley to sign with me even though this was my first real publishing opportunity; and my family, who encouraged me to stay with it when the work seemed overwhelming. Thank you all.

Introduction

My editor, Kevin Commins, and I were in the company conference room having a discussion about new book ideas. He wanted to publish a quality book on trading rules and had seen the 50 rules my company had published on its web site as a great starting point. Could we expand those basic ideas and produce a book on trading rules?

The owners were interested but really didn't have the time to commit. I told Kevin that the reason so few good books on trading rules were out there is because trading rules are more like guidelines and completely subjective; in my opinion most of the rules don't work anyway because most traders don't know how to use them. He was surprised to hear that point of view, but he was open to seeing something different. We discussed the concept a bit, and that became the basis for this book—answering the question, "Why don't the rules work?"

I discovered that is not an easy question to answer. For the first few months I had notes all over my home and office but nothing you could call a manuscript. After giving it substantial thought, I decided on a pathway of sorts to offer the reader a fair answer to "Why don't the rules work?"

At the core level, all the trading rules, guidelines, trader maxims, or insights are a factor of trader psychology and market psychology. The markets provide the illusion of unlimited opportunity and complete freedom to pursue it; "rules" and behavior controls seem to be in opposition to that idea. It is only after we as traders get beaten up by the markets for a period of time do we begin to have the light go on. "Cut your losses" is not a rule, it is a point of view that leads to protecting yourself. But what exactly does that mean for me personally, and why do I need protection from myself? Why don't I follow the rules?

In Edgar Allan Poe's short story "The Purloined Letter," he tells of a thief who has outwitted the best efforts of the police to recover a stolen document. As the story unfolds it becomes apparent to one of the outside observers that the letter must be hidden in plain sight; otherwise the police would have found it by that time seeing as no effort was spared in ransacking the home of the thief, nor was it ever found by his direct arrest and search. Working from this hypothesis, this observer was able to retrieve the stolen letter on his second visit to interview the thief; the letter was indeed "hidden in plain sight."

The rules of trading are much like that stolen letter. We often accept the various rules that have been taught to us as traders, but the psychology behind those rules is so inherently assumed that we overlook it. The psychology that really makes those rules work is often hidden in plain sight. As traders, we all would agree that properly applying the rules will help us better achieve consistent trading success, and we all know from personal experience that breaking the rules has cost us money in the markets. None of us want to admit we break the rules (and some of us don't even want to admit we *need* rules). So why don't we follow the rules?

The purpose of this book is to outline the deeper psychology behind most of the accepted trading rules and provide you, the individual trader, a better understanding of how to make your rules work. The rules are actually guidelines grouped into four separate parts; the underlying, basic psychology of each individual part is explored as each rule guideline is shown in proper context. As most traders know, there are literally unlimited ways of interpreting price action, choosing execution points, or formulating a hypothesis of general market conditions or potential price action. The intention is not to provide you with another trading system— God knows there are enough of those—but rather provide you a way of showing you two things to improve your trade approach: how you think and how the market thinks.

When you stop and realize that most traders have net losses, yet we all know the rules, what could possibly be the defining factor that separates the winning trader from the losing trader? I believe that there is no clear and definitive answer to that, other than one trader consistently follows the rules he has adopted for himself and the other trader doesn't; or worse yet has no rules. Because there is an unlimited number of ways to participate, I think the crucial issue is to find a way to personally apply the rules in a unique way that will work for you, and then do it all the time. It's easy to say "Cut your losses," but every trader will have a different way of defining that for themselves. The purpose of this book is to help you better define your personal trade approach by helping you interpret and apply the rules in a way that will work for your trading style. The rules are not the problem; it is making the rules work *for you* that is the problem.

HOW THIS BOOK IS ORGANIZED

The first step is getting a firm grip on exactly what you are doing when you participate. Part I, "Getting in the Game," outlines the psychology of market price action, what that can only mean as far as your trade selection is concerned, and how to begin from the point of a strong market presence. Trading is not as simple as "buy low–sell high" it is learning to understand the how and why behind price movement and how to participate proactively without letting prices make your decision for you. You must buy weakness and sell strength to successfully trade, even if another trader would call that "picking tops or bottoms." Your trade plan is a critical part of developing a mind-set that *uses* prices rather than *reacting* to them. Part of this process is learning to think in terms of probabilities, because no trading approach can be 100% accurate 100% of the time; that is not realistic for anyone. So Part I details what the game really is and how you can better participate from a more unbiased point of view.

Part II is "Cutting Losses." Every trader has had losses, and every trader still participating every day will tell you how important cutting losses is for the long-term health of a trading account. In this section we explore the underlying psychology of the rules of self-protection and why it is so hard to enforce this much-needed protection for ourselves. Many traders have a subconscious need to be "right" and will not liquidate a losing trade quickly. Even if you are not one of those traders, you will have something in your personal trade approach that makes it difficult to cut losses quickly under certain conditions. Developing a set of personal trade rules uniquely designed for your trading style will help you protect yourself—even when it is emotionally difficult to do so. Sooner or later, you will meet your Waterloo if you have failed to develop and enforce rules designed for your protection. Knowing when you are setting yourself up for a loss, and what to do if you are already in the market when you discover that fact, is a huge part of cutting losses. Sometimes your protection strategy will dictate that it is simply better not to trade. Having all these options clear in your trade approach is half the battle.

Part III explores the opposite dynamic: "Letting Profits Run." Every trader at one time or another has liquidated a winning trade, only to see that trade continue farther and farther in his favor. By applying a simple rule or two to remain in a winning trade, that trader might have taken a huge win from the market. Letting a profit run involves different things for each trader, but the underlying psychology is the same for everyone. Learning to develop an ever-expanding rule structure can help you hold your winners until the market has run out of potential in your favor; and that is rarely a function of price. Rather, it is related to the *net order flow* behind the price. Knowing when order flows are running out of potential for a winning trade is more important than the price at which it happens. Tracking this will involve multiple time frames, so a solid understanding of how those time frames are interrelated will help you write personal rules to maximize a winning trade.

Part IV is "Trading Maxims." In Part IV we look at the some of the most common trading rules and how they have both negative and positive psychological implications. Some of these rules will simply not work for you personally, but because they make sense initially you might be tempted to adopt them into your trade approach. This is frustrating at best and self-destructive at worst. Some of these trade rules work best only under certain market conditions and should be used only under those conditions or not at all. The underlying problem with most of these rules is that while they all sound good at first, they are often misunderstood in relation to time frames or the psychology of your personal trade approach. Sometimes they are simply in conflict with your overall style.

For example, the trading rule "Buy the strongest member of the complex" is not a rule that would work well for a day trader. This rule was originally used by position traders attempting to diversify across the underlying strength of something like the grain complex. Not knowing which of the grains may advance farthest for the underlying bullish scenario, traders would buy all of them and leverage a little farther in the strongest potential performer. In this case, anticipating a drought, they would buy corn, soybeans, and wheat but buy a bit more soybeans because soybeans traditionally will move several dollars a bushel more during a drought than corn or wheat might. If you are not trading for the pull in the grains under those conditions, a modest correction in the soybeans will most likely take you out or cause a loss on the buy side, because soybeans have traditionally been subject to extreme volatility, more so than corn or wheat. Buying the break for a day trade (in the strongest performer) could easily be the worst move possible for a day trader if that market went offer shortly after your entry. In that illustration, the trade rule doesn't work.

I'm not suggesting that you refrain from using a rule that you find valuable, but I think a solid understanding of what the rule was developed for, how successful traders use it, and whether your time frame could use it as well is a great way to determine if you could make that rule work for you personally.

In the final analysis, making the rules work is really about knowing your personal psychology and your market's psychology well enough that you do two things every day: Limit your potential to hurt yourself, and maximize your market's potential to pay you. Knowing the underlying psychology behind the rules will help, as well as personal study to apply them properly. During the time of your trader development you will most likely come to the same conclusion most successful traders have: The rules are unique to each trader, but every trader follows the same guidelines. All of the various rules, insights, guidelines, and trader maxims work together to do two things: prevent the trader from hurting himself, and allow the trader to get paid the most for his approach.

BEFORE YOU BEGIN

Before we get started, I would like to illustrate how this understanding helped me improve my personal trade approach. As a young trader, I would often shoot from the hip—I would make a snap judgment based on my point of view and execute instantly. Because I had no real rules for execution, I did my share of jumping the gun on trades that eventually would have worked from that side, had I waited. Once I learned to follow Rule #10, "Keep good records and review them," I discovered that I was often correct on my initial observation about net price action, but being a day or two early (breaking Rule #4, "Know your time frame") I was often stopped out for a loss just before the market would turn. After this happened several times, I would simply execute again immediately at my stop price for a reentry, resulting in another small loss as my tighter but deeper stop was elected (breaking Rule #7, "Your first loss is your best loss"). This would happen six or seven times (breaking Rule #9, "Don't overtrade") as the market went a significant distance against my original execution; then the market would turn. I would hold the winner but I would need to overcome a major loss to my equity before the trade had a net gain. On a 200-point move in Japanese yen, for example, I would net only 30 to 40 points because I had a 150-point deficit to overcome first.

After reviewing my notes, my observations, and my execution history, I decided that my skill at observing a trade was not the issue. My timing was usually a day or two early. I made a new rule for myself: "If I have three losses in a row, I cannot trade for 24 hours." If my first three attempts to buy what I felt was a sell-off were losers, usually I would get another chance right in the same area or better within a day or so. By disciplining my execution in this manner, I would save myself three or four more losers, finally obeying the rules in Part II, and then I was often able to use the rules in Part III. Nothing really changed in my trade selection or my analysis, but following the rules better allowed me to get into position better and *stay* there better. I learned to make the rules work for me personally. The money to be made was always there.

PART I

Getting in the Game

Know
Your Game

The longest journey begins with the first step.
— Lao Tzu, in the *Tao te Ching*

A key to making the rules work is an understanding of the psychology behind the rules, knowing where they work best, and knowing if that is congruent with our personal trading style. The psychology behind the rule is what it is, in part, because the psychology of the market itself is what it is. I don't think we can make our rules work at their best without a solid understanding of this underlying market psychology.

Critical to that assessment is understanding our own personal psychology. No matter where you personally are on the scale of trader evolution or your application of your developing skills, you will eventually discover that your own personal psychology is by far the single most important variable to your lasting success as a trader. Indeed, only a trader who accepts this point of view about his own psychology will be able to successfully make his trading rules work—because the rules are self-created, self-enforced, and self-defeating. Without a solid grasp of both market psychology and personal psychology, your results will most likely be net losses, even if you have a winning systematic approach and good rules.

Regardless of your current level of sophistication or trading background, there is one indisputable fact about the underlying structure of trading markets that you need to thoroughly understand before you place yourself at risk. Futures, options on futures, and cash foreign exchange

3

(FOREX), the markets most readers will be trading are all *zero-sum markets*. The price action and cash management take place in an environment where no money is ever made or lost; gains or losses accrue as a cash debit or credit between accounts on deposit after trades are cleared. In other words, a winning trade is paid its cash credit from the exact opposite losing trade. The clearing corporation of the exchange simply assigns a cash credit to the account with the winning trade and assigns a cash debit to the account with the losing trade.

In the final analysis, it is the losers who pay the winners. You cannot accrue a cash credit increase in your trading account unless some other trader (or group of traders) somewhere, trading through the same exchange with you in the same market, has lost the exact same amount. In order for you to make $10,000 from your trading, someone else (or a group of someone elses) had to lose $10,000. You can't participate in zero-sum trading without accepting that risk.

It is the very nature of zero-sum transaction trading that makes using and applying trade rules so critical to lasting success. If you personally don't know enough about what you are doing, or the risk you are really taking, you will be the loser who pays some other winning trader. The market does not function any other way.

Let's take a look at the psychology behind price action. I believe this is much deeper than the simple fact that for every winning trade there is a loser. Zero-sum trading presents some fascinating insights into crowd behavior and what is really needed or required to exploit price action profitably. Let's start with the basics:

Buyer→ $2.33 ←Seller

You enter a buy order to open a position in corn at $2.33/BU. In order for you to receive a fill on your buy order, it must be matched against a sell order at that price. For the sake of illustration, let's assume there is also a sell order to open a position. Therefore, two separate traders have put themselves at risk, and a new long position and a new short position are now active. What happens next?

Another set of orders comes in, and those are matched, but if at that moment there is an imbalance in the order flow, the market is requoted to reflect the imbalance. In other words, if there are more buy orders left over after the sell orders are matched, the market ticks higher and is matched with sell orders at higher prices, if they are there. The remaining buy orders are then matched at that new higher price. If there are more buy orders left over again, another tick higher results.

Of course, this illustration is conceptual. As most traders know, those buy and sell orders are constantly coming in and are combinations of stop orders, limit orders, and market orders from both sides; the mix is always changing. What we are concerned with is the pressure on the price as the *net* order flow is processed from one moment to the next. If the order imbalance remains on the buy side, the market will continue to tick higher until the imbalance is corrected and the buy/sell orders are about evenly matched again. If, at that point, the sell orders overwhelm the buy orders, the market will begin to tick lower and will continue to do so until the buy and sell orders again become about evenly balanced with the sell orders. The ebb and flow of price action comes from these order imbalances, and what we call an *uptrend* or *downtrend* is in reality a net imbalance lasting for some period of time.

So let's assume after a period of time, the net order imbalance for that period of time has resulted in a new price for corn at that point:

$$\rightarrow \$2.38/\text{BU} \leftarrow$$

Your open-trade *long* now has a profit of \$0.05 per bushel. The open *short* from your executed order (the other trader speculating) has an open-trade loss of exactly the same \$0.05 per bushel. If, at that exact moment, both of you choose to liquidate your positions, and your orders offset each other at that point, your account will be credited and his account will be debited the exact same dollar amount (less any fees, of course).

This is all easily understandable, but there is a completely other world at work in that process. That other world is the psychology of the traders involved and how that creates their urge to action resulting in them placing the orders in the first place.

What is not immediately apparent in price action is *perception*—how that net credit or debit is affecting the account holder, what that account holder is thinking, and what he must do next. What is certain is that at some point, both traders must liquidate; no one can stay in the market forever. When the losing position is liquidated at some point, the losing trader must do an equal but opposite trade against himself. In other words, if I have bought the market, and prices are moving lower, I must sell to liquidate my loss, adding power to the dominant force in control of the market at that point. My mental and emotional state is in direct conflict with my desire for a profit, and my only choice really is to liquidate now or risk a bigger loss. If I "wait it out" I am trying to anticipate the market will reverse and eventually show a profit on the trade for me (thereby making a loser out of the original short who initially had the open-trade profit).

But all of this thinking or emotion is going on inside my mind and has nothing to do with what is driving the market. In order for prices to advance or decline, there must be more orders on that side of the market.

Prices can advance only if there are more buy orders than sell orders at that moment. Prices can decline only if there are more sell orders than buy orders at that moment. How that order flow personally affects my account balance or my emotional state does not concern the net order-processing function of the market. In any attempt to profit from any perceived opportunity in a zero-sum transaction market, you simply must be on the right side of the eventual net order flow from that moment forward until you liquidate. If you are on the wrong side of the net order flow, you will have an open trade loss until you liquidate.

None of what happens inside the mind of the trader during that time can affect the market in any way; it can only affect the net balance controlled in some way by the trader in some way. This is why you *must* have rules and know how to follow them. You cannot know for certain until later, after you enter your position, whether you are on the right side of the net order flow.

The important thing to remember is that there is an emotional pressure at work in most traders that will influence their perception of price action. They all entered their trades expecting to win, but in most cases they will have to consider liquidating at a loss. All of the emotional or psychological stress involved in trading boils down to "When do I get out?" Because the owner of the winning position has a lead on the market, he is under less of this stress than the loser. In most cases, when the pain of holding the losing hand gets too big for the losing trader, he will liquidate in the same direction as the winning position. A simple example is a market slowly advancing higher as more buy orders overwhelm the sell orders, until the market hits the liquidating buy stops above the market placed by the sellers who are holding a losing position. The market now advances further on that buying pressure.

None of the above-described background to price action has anything to do with market study, risk control, trading systems, or technical analysis. It has to do only with the fact that if you are going to be in the market, you run the risk that you will be on the wrong side of the order flow. What does that do to the trader's emotions? What will he do? What will *you* do?

Because you cannot profit consistently in a zero-sum market unless you are on the correct side of the order flow, your entire analysis and trade plan must take into consideration some way to identify where the order flow is and what to do if you are on the wrong side of it. The issue of cutting losses is essentially to have some method of negating any emotional conflict created by a losing trade, in such a way that you will not hesitate to get out of the way of the actual order flow if you are on the wrong side of it. Part of how you participate on your trade, regardless of your unique approach to finding a trade opportunity, must always answer the question: "Where is the order flow?"

Most of the studies done on net trader performance come to the inescapable conclusion that around 90% of traders will close their accounts at a net loss. None of those traders expected to lose, and yet they did. Part of their losses came from the emotional conflict created in their minds when the market moved against them, creating pressure on their execution. Every trader has had the frustration of finally throwing in the towel and liquidating his position, only to see the market reverse shortly thereafter and prices move favorably, if only he had stayed in. All that really happened is that the order flow dried up in one direction and then turned the other way. For that particular trader it resulted in a net loss to his account. That particular trader will now be tempted to "just ride it out" on the next trade until prices eventually return. Of course, the one time this doesn't happen will result in a total loss in the account. It only takes one "just ride it out" to ruin that particular trader.

To avoid being that trader, and to master the game of successful speculation, you must know what you are really capitalizing on when you identify a trade opportunity. You *must* accept and trade from the point of view: "Where is the order flow?" and you must have a method of getting out of the way when you are not on the right side of the order flow. All the analysis or study you could ever do *must* answer these two central questions.

One assumption you can make to know your game is that most traders do not know the game they are playing. About 80 to 90% of price action is simply the losers liquidating their losing trades. When you begin each day, and before you place a trade, ask yourself this question: "Where is the loser?"

In the final analysis, the game you are playing is "Beat the Loser." The great trader J. P. Morgan said it best: "Anyone who is unaware of the fool in the market probably *is* the fool."

Have a Trading Plan

If you fail to plan, you plan to fail.

—Old wisdom

I have had the privilege of seeing almost everything there is to see in the business of trading. I have met some very well-known traders, big names in business or finance; I've been on several trading floors, visited the trading pits numerous times, worked side-by-side with some tremendously successful market participants, and seen all the catastrophes, mayhem, blowouts, and financial blunders capable of novice traders. I have asked all the right questions and all the wrong questions. In my experience, I have to say that there was very little critical difference between the net winning traders and the net losing traders in most areas. All of them had good understanding of basic market fundamentals, used a solid technical analysis or research of some kind, and exercised a lot of personal discipline.

The one thing that stood out, the one thing that separated the net winner from the net loser, all things being equal, was that the net winner had a trading plan in addition to his other skills. The net winner knew he was up against not just the market and his competitors, but he was up against himself, too. To guard against the possibility that he (the trader) could blow himself out of the water at any time if he wasn't careful, that trader had a plan.

A trading *plan* is different from a trading *system*. A trading system is designed to find an inequality in the market and offer a better buy or sell entry than at some other time. A trading plan takes into account what happens *after* that. Once we have identified what we think is an opportunity, it is how we participate from that point forward that makes all the difference. A trading plan will address and complement a systemized approach much better if it is seen as an equally important part of a strong market presence.

A trading plan addresses the parts of trading that are most fully in your control. For example, when and where you do your market study or analysis; when and where you place or move a stop-loss order; when you take a trading break—basically anything that involves you taking action or not taking action, independent of the actual market itself, is spelled out in a trading plan.

A trading system is only designed to exploit perceived inequalities in the market, but it can never be 100% accurate or find exactly where every potential "top" or "bottom" is in the time frame you are working with. If a system could do that, no other discussion of rules would be needed. Once you have executed and placed yourself at risk, you have moved into the area of your system's probabilities and limitations. You as an individual cannot extend control over price action; you can only control how you use price action or how you participate in price action. Once the trade is taken, the "die is cast" so to speak. Whether you win or lose at that point is completely out of your control.

Because your system is not capable of finding each and every turn there is to profit from in real time, a trading plan is needed to prevent you as a trader from getting reckless or from placing yourself in lower-probability trades, and what to do when the unexpected happens. A trading plan needs to address your particular trading strengths and weaknesses; it in no way diminishes the need for a systemized methodology, nor is it designed to replace one.

Your trading plan can be followed 100% of the time because it is an expression of the sum total of what your rules are designed to create; it controls your behavior, which is a function of discipline and willingness to follow those rules. Your trading system may never be more than around 55% predictive in finding winning trades, but you can follow your trading plan's rules 100% of the time. When your trading system is wrong, your trading plan will help you minimize the loss. When your trading system is right, your trading plan will help you maximize the gains.

A qualified trading plan is both concise and flexible. It adapts to market conditions as needed and is concerned with protecting the trader. You can think of a trading system as strategic and a trading plan as tactical. To use a military illustration, "winning the war" is the goal, strategy involves finding the enemy's weakness, and tactics are how you exploit that weakness.

Think of your trading system or methodology as a strategic attempt to consistently find a weakness in the market and exploit it. It really doesn't matter what it is; it simply needs to be consistent. Your trading plan is more like the "if–then" tactical response to conditions as they change in real time and as you learn more about a particular trade's potential as it develops. Your trading system is designed to help you find the edge; your trading plan is designed to help you keep your edge or recognize when you don't have it at a particular moment.

Your trading plan is where your rules are used to maximize your winning advantage when you have it and minimize your losses when you don't. What is *never* in question is that winning the war involves both strategy and tactics; sometimes tactics save the strategy, and sometimes the strategy needs very little tactics. Knowing this balance is also important because, as we discuss later, all analysis of the markets will have a strategic advantage but also a strategic limitation. Your trading plan gives you the tactical advantage of knowing which strategy will work best, under which conditions, and what is most likely to be your best initial move to keep pushing your advantage into more and more profitable positions. The major goal is, of course, to cut losses and let profits run.

SO HOW DO I CREATE A SOUND TRADING PLAN?

Every trader must make several critical distinctions when creating a sound trading plan. We discuss some of the more crucial aspects in greater detail throughout each rule in the book but there are several initial ones you can focus on to start creating your unique trading plan. Starting from the assumption that you can't participate at all if you lose too much of your trading capital, the first concern is how to minimize your participation when you are losing. This is different than cutting your losses. Cutting losses is part of your trading system and after you have had a significant amount of those individual losses for you personally it is time to consider a few things. First, are you using the system or methodology correctly? Part of your trading plan should be a regular reassessment of whether you are fudging on the system in some way. Are you taking trades the system wouldn't take? Are you hesitating on taking every signal? Are there some trades in there that you waited on and were "late"?

A solid trading plan is a guideline to help you maintain focus. Your first and best clue that you are not maintaining your best trading focus is a series of losses that are outside the limits of the trading systems' probabilities. At that point, you as the trader must decide what your rules are when you are experiencing an irregular drawdown. Some of the better things to do include taking a step back and observing if the market itself is operating in a manner that is no longer consistent with the trading system or method hypothesis. If you are using a trend-following strategy, suppose the market is no longer trending? A trend-following system will get chopped to pieces during a period of consolidation. What is your plan for a tactical change at such a time? Only you can answer that question completely but the theme of your trading plan must consider a "what if" scenario for the outside chance that the quality of the market has changed enough to lower the probability of your system performing. Part of your trade plan is some method of standing aside.

There are times in every trader's life when the worst possible thing that trader could do is participate. Your trading plan should address the possibility that outside life issues or pressures can influence your ability to trade well. What can you do to protect yourself when your emotional or mental sharpness is potentially dropping? When you lose control of your focus, you run the risk of missing a critical piece of information about the market structure at just the wrong point, creating a loss. Your trading plan must address your personal and emotional needs as well as the financial risks you are taking. It might be a good idea to plan regular trading breaks from time to time, regardless of how you are doing in the markets. If you are planning a major life event such as getting married or sending one of your children off to college for the first time, your trading plan should address those needs in such a way that will prevent you from getting careless. All traders at some point have had something throw them off, and if they continued trading at that point, in most cases that stress or pressure affected them negatively as far as their trade selection and execution are concerned.

Everyone has heard the stories of the lucky individual who won a large amount of cash in a state lottery. Suddenly, without any advance warning, some fortunate soul has several million dollars in cash. Being completely unprepared for such an event, many of these people have made serious financial mistakes with those monies and in the end, were worse off financially than before they had won that money. Your trade plan should also address how to participate best if you are doing well at some point. A large degree of financial success can have a negative impact on a trader just as easily as large losses can.

To ensure your continued success it would be wise to adopt some method of reducing your participation until you have mentally and emotionally processed that success. There is a temptation to think that what created your success and the size of that success can easily be duplicated and will always be the state of your trading. This happens a lot to new traders with little experience who, unbeknownst to them, were just lucky.

They make a large amount of cash by accident and confuse that with true trading skill—or worse, think they have found the perfect system. If they are not careful, their lack of skill will cause this trader to "give it all back plus more." Additionally, this trader will not be sensitive to the possibility that the quality of the market has changed and his "system" is no longer effective, nor will he know when it might become effective again. Your trading plan should address what to do when you are far enough ahead to create a possible problem for yourself. In other words, what do you do if your money gets "bigger than your head"?

If you are thinking along these lines, you are beginning to draw the conclusion that all of the rules we discuss here, together as a group, are where your trade plan initially comes from. In the final analysis, your trading plan is a reflection of your willingness to properly use the rules when you need controls on your behavior. Your rules can change and your trading plan can continue to evolve, but your willingness to consider your side of the ledger equally as important as your trading system is the key to writing an effective trade plan. Following is an example of what I would consider to be a well-written trading plan.

> *My goal is to earn 100% on my trading equity before the end of the year. To maintain my focus I will set a near-term goal every quarter to be at a 25% gain and I will plot my equity daily. If I reach my quarterly goal ahead of the last trading day of the quarter I will take a two-day break. I will hold any open positions that are at a profit but any open trade losses I will close at that point before I take a break.*
>
> *If my open-trade gains continue into the new quarter I will add to those winning positions by a factor of 25%. I will move my protective stops up to reduce my exposure on the entire position.*
>
> *If I am behind on my trade goal for the quarter, I will take a five-day break. I will reevaluate my trade system and ask the question: "Has my market quality changed to something in which my system is not able to perform at its best?"*
>
> *During the year I will not trade more than three markets. I have learned I cannot focus well on more than three markets at a time.*
>
> *If I have more than four losing trades in a row in any of my three markets I will take a trading break for five days. Again, I will leave open position winners alone in the other markets but close all losing positions. I will again roll protective stops to reduce my risk.*
>
> *When I take a trading break, I will enter resting limit orders in the open-trade winners to take the objective profit should I be unavailable and the market reaches those levels during my break.*

If I am ahead of my plan for the year at any point I will take a break. I will take 30% of the new equity out of my account and place that into a secure place. If I am behind I will not add equity under any circumstances. If I reach a 40% drawdown from my high equity I will quit for the year.

I will record my daily trade activity in my trading log and review this weekly. I will know my ratios and results; I will look to improve them by 5% each quarter.

I will trade only from the bull side because my analysis tells me that all three of the markets I have selected have more than a year of solid bullish fundamentals. I will learn how to use options this year because I see from last year I could have protected more trades if I had a solid grasp of when to use options and when not to. I will invest two hours a week on option knowledge.

My son is leaving for Europe in May. I will not trade the week before he leaves or the week after. I plan to join him in the fall for Oktoberfest for one week and will not trade the three days before I leave or when I get back. I know I suffer from jet lag so the week after I am back I am not at my best. I have blocked out these times on my trade calendar so I will not be tempted to trade anyway.

This was an actual trade plan written by a friend of mine who trades E-mini futures. He uses a simple technical approach and has a very thorough risk control method. His trading plan addresses the need for 100% personal discipline. Notice that it makes no mention of the technical approach he uses. The approach is his strategy. His plan specifies how to maximize his side of the equation—the tactical advantage he personally needs.

When developing your own trading plan, remember that your systemized methodology won't have 100% winners no matter how you slice it. The one thing you always have 100% control over is your participation. Your trading plan should focus on your participation, not your execution.

RULE #3

Think in Terms of Probabilities

There is an ambush everywhere from the army of accidents; therefore the rider of life runs with loosened reins. . . .

—Hafiz

Because we live in a world where often certain things appear to be commonplace and "normal," we have developed a greater feeling of certainty as it pertains to our daily lives. Human beings find a sense of certainty in the belief that our day-to-day world is natural and is simply the way things are. Some of us have grown so accustomed to this feeling that we have a routine that actually bores us, and some of us go out of our way to do something, anything, to break free of the grip of the ordinary in our lives.

Often when the unexpected happens, we feel that the odds are somehow changed, but this is usually seen as temporary. Often the truly random nature of things is not regularly apparent enough for us to see that whatever happened could have occurred at any time and that we are at risk in that manner at all times every day. For example, because most people will be in a car wreck perhaps only once in their lives, the everyday risk of driving seems to be very low. If we do have a car wreck, we consider it a "random" event that only seemed manifested to us "by accident." We feel this way because normally we drive every day without incident. We have come to feel that it is more of a certainty that each day will pass without the random event occurring to us personally. If it does occur, we think it is a fluke.

The fact is, most people create the "accident" that they find themselves in by failing to make the connection between their actions and what happens next. For example, most people who drink and drive don't believe the problem was entirely theirs, yet it was their impaired judgment that increased the odds that the seemingly random event would happen to them. Because they drive sober and without incident 95% of the time, they fail to recognize that during the 5% of the time they are not sober, the previous 95% success rate is now null and void. The rules of the game have changed. They are in an entirely different environment that bears no resemblance at all to the previous degree of certainty.

Our mistake is not so much in our perception of reality, but in understanding the nature of how probabilities affect us all day, every day. There are very few things in life that involve certainty, and the fact that some things only happen to each of us individually maybe once in our lives does not change the probability that they will happen every day to someone.

Indeed, the entire business of actuary analysis is an attempt to analyze how best to spread the risk of an event that *will* happen across as many people as possible to whom it *might* happen. Insurance companies make money by diluting the risk in this way, and they do best by writing policies to people to whom the event will almost certainly never happen. As an example, the reason active scuba divers pay much more in life insurance premiums is that a certain percentage of scuba divers will drown each year. If you don't scuba-dive, your risk of accidental drowning is lower; therefore your premiums are lower. But the fact is, *someone* will drown this year, and the odds that are a regular percentage of those people will be scuba divers. Ask scuba divers what they think of that risk and all of them will most assuredly say, "Not me . . . I don't do anything stupid when I dive." Those divers have a sense of certainty that "drowning won't happen to *me*."

This issue of perception regarding certainties and probabilities changes completely when we begin trading. We leave the comfort of a world that usually works a certain way and enter into a world where the truly random and unexpected can happen at any time. The events are random and unexpected not because the market is indefinable or because price action is somehow so mysterious as to defy explanation, but because we as individual traders cannot possibly know everything about the market at all times; therefore we have a percentage of risk that is certain. Reducing this risk is not about more study or more knowledge. Reducing this risk is about knowing probabilities.

All attempts to profit from a trade are in reality a best guess regarding future price action. It really doesn't matter what your methodology is or which technical or fundamental approach you ultimately settle on as the right combination of risk/reward system right for you. Because the nature of trading markets involves risk and uncertainty, it is impossible to know exactly how any one trade will eventually play out through price action until it gets there. Markets are not definable past a certain point, and no matter the depth or scope of pretrade analysis or research, there is always the possibility that prices won't respond in the anticipated direction or won't respond in a time frame you are willing to trade in. Wall Street and LaSalle Street are full of traders who were right too soon, waited too long, got out too soon, got in too late, and so on. All of those kinds of results— whether this means small profits, no profits, small losses or big losses— are simply because whatever systematized approach was being relied upon had reached its unique limit or the trader failed to appreciate that limit. They were all "best guesses," and that means they don't work 100% of the time to begin with.

Reducing your options to the best probability before you enter a trade is a function of several things. First, if you have done a proper assessment of general conditions according to your trade plan, there will be a point where prices are more favorable for an entry and will respond by an advance in the direction of conditions. Waiting for that point and then executing immediately is your best option, but where is that point?

When entering a trade we don't have the benefit of knowing if our execution point was the best price area; we find out sometime later. To improve your odds of timing your entry better, develop a series of "if–then" scenarios and ask yourself which is more likely.

Let's take an example from a potential bullish market condition. We could start with the hypothesis, "If conditions are bullish, and the trading population responds accordingly, then prices should rise." I know that sounds overly simplistic, but let's look at the various psychological aspects of such a simple statement and how that could play out in day-to-day price action.

If prices are at the moment still declining, this means either most traders don't feel conditions are bullish just yet, shorts are still in control of the market, or some combination of short-term and long-term market players looking for an opportunity is such that so far the net order flow remains offers. Since in most cases the majority of traders will not see a change in conditions far enough in advance to buy into a declining market, nor will they hold a position for the time required to earn the largest gain from a change in trend, we can assume that the majority of traders are either still short the falling market, on the sidelines waiting to make a move on the short side, or executing regularly from both sides with various results to their accounts. But as far as you are concerned, buying into a declining market has a degree of risk; hence the old favorite rule, "Don't pick tops or bottoms."

The absolute best place at the lowest risk for a trade is at the top or bottom, but finding that point is where the issue of probabilities comes in. If you knew the market had bottomed, and you were willing to assume the risk that conditions were turning bullish, you would want to execute at your price *right now*. It is absolutely certain that sooner or later that market *will* bottom, but is the current bottom *a* bottom or *the* bottom? No matter your research or analysis, you cannot know that for certain until sometime later, so you must think in terms of probabilities. Let's look at an example, shown in Figure 3.1.

In this figure, prices are moving in a general sideways trend. This means that buying and selling pressure is about equally balanced, because a market cannot steadily advance or decline unless there are more orders net from one side or the other. At this point in time, both the profitable shorts and the potential longs are seeing two opposing things. For the profitable short, his risk is increasing because no further net price action

FIGURE 3.1 Nearest Futures Contract, CBOT Corn for July Delivery, as of December 2005

is favorable for additional profit; he must either cover or wait for the trend to resume. For the potential long, the lower the price goes the better the opportunity if the change in trend is coming eventually. The longer the market does not go down, the better the potential that the actual bottom is finally in place.

In both cases, a choice to enter a buy order is the only result, no matter when either side decides to do it. How those buy orders are now being absorbed by early long liquidating with a sell order is a great clue. If the buy orders are *mostly* late (old) shorts liquidating, a drop in open interest will result. The traders with the selling point of view are changing their minds. Figure 3.2 shows this well. Note the steady advance in corn prices after high volume and a drop in open interest from that point forward.

The study of volume and open interest (V/OI) is an entirely separate issue from the psychology of thinking in terms of probabilities. If you were looking at a potential bullish scenario developing and you knew that most traders were bearish or prices were still declining, at some point you

FIGURE 3.2 Nearest Futures Contract, CBOT Corn for July Delivery, as of April 2006

knew that would change sooner or later because it is not reasonable to expect corn prices to drop to zero; somewhere between zero and where they are now, there *will* be a bottom price. It is more likely that a bottom is forming when no one wants to sell the market anymore; it is too risky for an additional price decline as far as the shorts are concerned. The potential bulls see their risk dropping the farther the market goes lower, and at some point they will simply say "Wow! That market is *on sale!*" and buy. If that scenario develops to the point where the buy orders (both new longs getting in and the old shorts getting out) compete with the sell orders (late shorts getting in and early longs getting out), and a drop in open interest results, the probabilities are rising that a bottom is forming because the only trade group who is most at risk for a price rise would be the open-trade winning shorts. The late short is dead meat anyway so he doesn't count.

When these two opposing points of view *actually do something*, you have the potential of a bottom forming at that price area. The V/OI ratio is only one clue. As a trader thinking in terms of probabilities, your only question is what is more likely to develop as time goes on. Sooner or later the market would have bottomed anyway. If you want to be on the right side for the pull when the trend changes, you have to ask yourself when and where it is most likely to happen, and that is not at any one price; it is a factor of the psychology behind the price.

The same psychology is behind every form of trade selection you do. You are looking for what is most likely, given your understanding of the bullish and bearish pressures that are playing out, as you understand them. If your time frame is shorter or longer, there will still be a more likely scenario that needs to be considered when you make your trade analysis. It needs to be considered as part of your trade plan because a flexible trade plan accounts for the possibility that something is changing. Your goal as a trader is to go with the path of least resistance, and that is a factor of probabilities, not analysis.

I have found that the best thing to do when I am looking for the true potential of a trade is to argue the case from both sides. I ask open-ended questions: Who is winning? Who is losing? What could make either side quit? What will cause the bulls or bears to liquidate? What will cause them to commit themselves more fully? Then the big question: Which is more likely?

By asking several kinds of questions designed not to form a certain absolute conclusion but to uncover the market's *best* probability forward, you as a trader have more options open to your trade selection process. As that trade selection process gets better and better defined over time, you will see that some trades are better for you personally than others. By thinking in probabilities you reduce the potential to have a loss by not taking low-probability trades, and you increase the potential to let profits run when you are in a high-probability trade. You can't know for certain ahead of time, but you can see the likelihood of one situation developing better than another.

At that point, you take your position and wait.

Know Your Time Frame

There is no right way to do something wrong.
—Anonymous

No discussion of trading would be complete without some dialogue regarding the issue of a trading time frame. There is a relationship between you as a trader, your trading plan, your trading methodology, and the amount of time all of these variables need to either confirm or deny that an opportunity for a profit exists. Not all methods will work under all time frames and if you personally don't know your own decision-making process very well, you might be tempted to work with a system that is not compatible with your natural time frame.

Everyone has a natural time frame in which they function best. By "natural time frame" I mean the amount of time required for you *personally* to reach a conclusion and then act on it. You cannot participate in the markets without reaching some sort of conclusion that prices are too high or too low relative to some other price that the market will eventually reach, assuming that your hypothesis is the right one. After you reach that conclusion, you then act on it. Depending on your personal temperament, your tolerance for risk, your previous success or failure, your education, and so on, the amount of time you need *personally* might vary, and this is what gives rise to the multitude of different trading approaches.

What is not immediately apparent to most traders is that what sounds good or makes sense initially when trying to create a market presence may not be compatible with their natural time frame. If this kind of conflict develops, then following the rules of the system will be difficult, as will trying to create a trading plan, because those things are not in harmony with the unique person of the individual trader.

The first step in selecting a methodology that will be best for you and in learning to best apply the rules is to select a trading time frame compatible with your character. If you are someone who likes to think things through from many different angles and then sleep on it before making a decision, a longer time frame for trading might work better—perhaps weeks or months. If you are someone who can make fast decisions and think on your feet, then a shorter time frame might be best for you. Most traders go through many different approaches and systems, not because they haven't found the right system, but because they haven't found the right system for *them*. In many cases, it is the issue of a compatible time frame that is a major factor.

Most traders start out trading in shorter time frames and then gradually expand to longer time frames. This is partly due to general inexperience and partly due to fear. Because gains or losses can occur quickly and sometimes appear to be random to new traders, a shorter time frame is attractive because it limits the amount of initial stress a new trader feels when he is learning to maintain or develop a market presence. Some traders conclude that trading is a completely random event and therefore they must trade a smaller time frame, such as minutes. Others feel that the markets must reflect actual supply and demand fundamentals sooner or later, and they view day-to-day or intraday fluctuations as random noise; they focus on remaining on one side of the market for months at a time.

If a trader selects a time frame too short to begin with, that trader typically feels that things are moving too fast and they tend to have a lot of hesitation at entry points, looking for confirmation before entering a position. Even a small correction can be frustrating because that was a loss that happened too fast, and often the market will return to the entry price quickly. If a trader selects a time frame too long for his temperament, the boredom of waiting for a trade to work over days or weeks will cause a desire to overtrade or try to force the market to pay him. The frustration of watching equity inhale and exhale daily by several thousand dollars will create a fear of loss and typically liquidation before the best objective is reached, because it is just taking too long to get there.

If you personally are experiencing a high degree of emotional conflict when you trade at this point, you can do a lot to eliminate that pressure by considering whether you are trying to trade a time frame that you personally are not compatible with. Additionally, if you have a high degree of expectation that a trade should work by a certain amount of time, you might be using the wrong time frame for you. Both of these inner experiences are good clues that you are not trading under your natural time frame.

FINDING CONGRUENCY IN YOUR TIME FRAME

Why do a natural time frame and a trading time frame need to be congruent? The simple answer is because that is how the market itself is structured. Every individual trader is operating under a unique world of bias, assumption, expectation, and emotion. Not one of those traders entered the market expecting to lose; they all (including you) are expecting their trade to make money "right now" when they put themselves into the market.

In order for that particular trade to either make money or lose money, a certain amount of time must pass—and every one of those traders can only give that trade so much time. The time between the execution to get into the market and the execution to exit the market is the *actual* time frame the individual trader is operating under; but that is often not the time frame he had planned on for himself.

Since most traders are experiencing losses, most traders feel a sense of attachment to their trades, and most traders are disappointed when any one trade is a loss; most traders are exerting force on the market in a time frame that is not what they intended. They all expected their trade to work "right now," but if the concept of "right now" is not exactly clear, then the amount of time required for the trade to develop its true potential is not clear. If the price action that is happening "right now" is not what the individual trader expected or intended, he loses control of his execution because the price action in the market is influencing his willingness to act. That trader is not choosing to make use of prices; the prices are using *him.*

A simple illustration of this potential is a successful long-term trader holding a position for weeks against him. If, for example, this trader is expecting a rise in prices, and he is willing to wait *months* for the potential to develop, he might buy that market on a weekly time frame. He knows that it is usually impossible to pick the actual day or hour the market will make the actual turn in price, but he also knows that when it does, he will be positioned near the best area for a price advance. He might buy part of his position at that time and plan on buying more over a six-week period of time. He may even buy part of his position at an actual lower price than his first execution because he is confident enough in his analysis and his trade plan to trust himself with that particular use of his capital. He might have committed himself to holding the position, no matter what, until a particular date forward because if it isn't happening by then, the potential in the trade is dropping. For this particular trader, on this time frame, what happens the day after his initial purchase is unimportant; he might see that as random noise. That particular trader's concept of the trade working "right now" is *six weeks long*.

Now consider a bearish trader in the exact same market. He might be looking at a weekly high as a selling opportunity, but he is using an hourly time frame and has no intention of holding any trade over a weekend. After that market trades to a weekly high, he might wait *six hours* for a confirmation that the high is in for the week. He then executes on the sell side, and if that trade is not working by the end of the day he will liquidate. This trader's time frame for "right now" is *two hours*. Additionally, if the trade is profitable he will exit the market within a very short time frame—by the weekend.

In both cases, no matter what time frame each trader is executing under, sooner or later the net order flow will affect their positions. In one case, *weeks* are needed for the corresponding pressure on the trader's thinking to develop; in the other case, only a few *hours*. The eventual price that market ends up at during the next three months probably won't matter to the hourly time frame trader; he will have had many opportunities as he would define them during that time. The weekly time frame trader might see things entirely different. Yet both traders are executing in the same market, and both traders exert pressure on price action by their execution.

WHICH TRADER ARE YOU?

Knowing your personal time frame is a necessary part of your trade approach because the only thing that will pay you a profit is getting on the right side of the order flow *for that time frame*. If you are an hourly trader, it is not wise to position yourself on the opposite side of the weekly trader. His order flow takes longer to develop, and he will not execute on the other side of the market until a much larger price swing has occurred. If you are selling against a weekly trader who is buying, he is willing to hold that trade much longer, whether the market moves for him or against him. He won't be there to sell off his unprofitable longs in the time frame you are looking to buy back a profitable short. Your $200-per-contract open-trade short is random noise to him. Consequently, if your trade is not working in a few hours and you want to liquidate your loser, he also won't be there to liquidate his open-trade profitable long—he intends to hold it for *months*.

Of course, this is an over-simplification of price action, and in any liquid market there will be plenty of orders available on either side. But the point is this: Different time frames are competing, and the intention of one time frame is not always the intention of another. Your best trades occur when your own time frame is the same as the time frame currently in control of the market at that point. When that changes, your trade is over.

Part of developing a sound trading plan and a strong market presence depends in part on knowing how to get positioned on the order flow as it develops for a particular time frame. To do this, you must know what your time frame is before you begin trading. If you are not willing to hold positions past a certain amount of time, your system or methodology must be compatible for that time frame. Don't buy a trend-following approach if you aren't going to stay in the market long enough to get paid from that trend; instead, maybe you should consider a volatility approach, one that will give a signal for liquidation in a shorter period of time.

A good rule of thumb is that your time frame should reflect your willingness to hold a winner, not your tolerance for risk. All systemized approaches or methodology must have an effective way to cut a loss quickly, but the ability to hold the winner is a factor of your time frame. If your time frame is daily, how many days could that trade have potential? Once you understand your personal time frame you can better hold your positions because all time frames have a period of time that they need to fully express their potential. Quite possibly that amount of time might be very similar to your natural tendency to allow things to develop for you, under your personal natural time frame.

To help determine that ideal amount of time, I have found that a factor of three seems to work best. If you execute on a weekly time frame, you could expect your trade's full potential to take around three weeks to develop, assuming you are seeing it right to begin with. If you are a 15-minute trader, expect your trade to need 45 minutes or so to develop. Of course, any one trade could have significantly more potential than your particular time frame will uncover, but that isn't really the issue. No matter what your time frame is, in every trade those probabilities drop after some period; how far that trade goes beyond your objective is an issue of using multiple time frames (see Rule #12).

But in all cases, whichever time frame you choose to use for your method, ask yourself if that method and time frame are something you are naturally comfortable with. If you don't like making snap decisions, then a short-time-frame approach offering several potential trades every day will probably not work well for you. If you can't stand waiting around for things to happen, then a methodology that requires months (such as a system heavily biased to the underlying fundamentals) may not be a good fit.

The important thing to remember when you select your time frame is that cutting losses is only part of it. Sooner or later you will get on the right side of the order flow, and when you are you need to know that it is okay to give that trade the full amount of time it needs to develop the actual potential it has. Your time frame is a significant part of that.

PART II

Cutting Losses

Define
Your Risk

Not risking is the surest way of losing. If you do not risk, risk eventually comes to you. There is simply no way to avoid taking a risk. If a person postpones taking risks, the time eventually comes when he will either be forced to accept a situation that he does not like or to take a risk unprepared.

—David Viscott, M.D.,
Commodity Trader's Almanac, 1989

It is my opinion that the single most important skill to develop as a trader is the dispassionate ability to cut losses. How you conclude is the best way for you personally is less important than having a way to do it and doing it all the time. Of all the trading traps that have to be avoided, the one trap that will cripple any trader the quickest is the inability to know and admit when the trade hypothesis is simply not working nor may it ever work. This goes much farther and deeper than "admitting I was wrong," believing "I can afford to wait a little before I decide what to do," "taking necessary heat until this turns around," or any number of ways of doing the same thing: justifying your inaction in the face of your equity evaporating.

The only reason a losing trade happens is because at *that precise moment* you are on the wrong side of the order flow. It really doesn't matter how that happened or what you told yourself in order to execute at that point; the fact is *you are losing money.* As long as you continue to remain on the wrong side of the order flow your loss will continue to grow, until either you are forced to liquidate (margin call or worse) or you choose to liquidate when the pain of the loss affects you so greatly you can't bear it anymore. In all cases of a loss being large and unbearable, the simple act of liquidating is done when the trader has lost control of his execution. Someone or something else—either the exchange, the broker, the margin clerk, or your personal need to avoid pain (emotion)—controls the net result now sitting in the trading account. The worst losses will always occur when you lose control of your liquidating execution.

This loss of control over your own money is not a trading issue. It is a symptom of a deeper problem that at its root cause is a factor of the trader's personal psychology. No matter what the root issue is, the potential for that root issue to take away your money *must* be adequately addressed and prepared for. Sooner or later you as a trader will break the one rule you simply cannot trade successfully without: Define your risk. If you trade without defining your risk of loss, it is only a matter of time before you find yourself in a trading situation you were unprepared for and money is leaving your account at a hypersonic pace. To avoid that potential you must master this most important rule of trading: Define your risk.

What does it mean to define your risk? In my view, it is not as simple as merely entering a protective stop order, although that goes without saying (I address stops in Rule #6). Defining your risk is a factor of your personality and your personal skill set. Defining your risk should include not just the cash dollar risk on each and every trade but should also be considered as part of your overall market presence and willingness to participate.

Not every trader is a good fit for all market conditions or even all market opportunities. As an example, just because you own a gas station and are intimately involved with the purchase and sale of gasoline every day does not mean that you would instantly understand all the important requirements for successfully trading in Harbor Unleaded Gasoline Futures (HU) at the New York Mercantile Exchange (NYMEX). Nor would you immediately comprehend HU's unique relationship to crude oil simply because you have read a brief discussion of the "crack spread" or attended a one-day seminar on "Using Candlestick Analysis in the Energy Complex." Many traders make the mistake of assuming that a general understanding of their personal business can provide them an adequate beginning edge to exploiting price action. Nothing could be further from the truth. In fact, the exact opposite is often the case, usually because the trader makes the assumption that his business knowledge is transferable to trading and therefore does not understand why his knowledge is not helping his trading.

One question you should ask when defining your risk is "How much do I really know about the _____ market?" If your honest answer is "Nothing, really," then it would be a very good idea to commit to learning a basic understanding of what traders in that particular market focus on and what tends to cause a reaction in prices. As an example, many traders are surprised to learn that the Producer Price Index (PPI) and Consumer Price Index (CPI) reports are often largely ignored by professional FOREX traders but are closely watched by interest rate traders, even though the two markets are intimately related on many levels. Without that knowledge, a novice trader might be tempted to execute a FOREX trade basing his choice on something the FOREX market hasn't considered tremendously valuable at this time, thereby assuming a potential risk that he wouldn't have had otherwise.

As a trader looking for the best market presence you can master, it is wise to consider your actual education process as part of your risk-reducing strategy. Can you honestly say that you are an expert on the market you trade? If not, part of knowing your risk might be to take a regular refresher course on market basics for the markets you trade. All markets evolve and change over time. What worked last year may not work this year. Be prepared to regularly review and supplement your market knowledge, because often the best way to define your risk is to know in advance where the potential pitfalls might be.

Additionally, defining risk can include an assessment of your personal financial condition and where that adds pressure to your life. This is different than the maxim, "Only trade with money you can afford to lose." If you are recovering from a divorce, for example, and have a strong need to recover financially, those non-market-related emotional pressures or conflicts might easily spill over into your trade execution for reasons that have nothing to do with actual trade potential. Someone who thinks he can make his house payment from trading and expects to make that money from the market in a short period of time may be placing himself in a worse position should he have even a small loss. Those types of risk can be very real and should be carefully considered along with the actual dollar risk you take when you establish a new position.

How does your spouse or significant other feel about your desire to trade? If your spouse thinks you are nuts for trading soybean futures, maybe you don't plan to tell your spouse you are losing until it is tax time and you have a brand-new deduction to discuss. Imagine the pressure on your relationship at that time. Maybe it would be a good idea for you to consider the input your spouse may have. Many traders have discovered that the critical component to their trading has been a sense of confidence that they are supported by their spouse. Some traders find sharing the wealth they have earned from the markets with their families has given them a better sense of achievement. But the essential element that is often overlooked by many traders is that their day-to-day relationship with their spouse can be both positively and negatively affected when the family finances are in question one way or the other. Having your spouse's full support will help you define your risk better if you are one of those traders who might have your focus broken by conflict in the home.

One thing you can count on: Certain times in a person's life make one less available for the strong emotional and personal focus required to successfully speculate. Be sensitive to the personal side of your trading and consider that there might be times when you will just not be at your best; those are the times to either stand aside or reduce your trade size for a period of time.

Once we have done enough of the right homework for the market we want to trade, and we have assessed our personal pressures enough to know we won't be negatively affected by them, we are ready to address the issue of the financial risks inherent in every market. The fact is, we could be wrong on our next trade and we might have to accept a cash dollar loss. No successful net winning trader has 100% winning trades. There is a tendency for some traders to subconsciously expect each individual trade to be the home run; otherwise, why are we in? Often it is this very expectation that causes us to make the mistake of not defining what dollar loss we are prepared to take in the event the trade is a loser. After all, why place a stop or select a getting-out point if this trade is the home run?

Many traders who have suffered larger-than-intended losses have looked back on how that happened and said, "Yes, I could have gotten out sooner *but* . . . (enter stupid reason here)." The unwillingness to define the risk ahead of time put them in a position where they had no plan in place to protect themselves; they lost control of their execution and now were at the mercy of the market. Instead of ruthlessly cutting the loss at a predefined point, they did something else. They hoped, prayed, waited, etc. and the end result is that the market kept marking their account lower until they had no choice.

In the final analysis, defining our risk is a method to cut our losses, simply because we refrain from putting ourselves at risk until we have addressed all the potential ways we could lose money to begin with. We are not going to let anything take money away from us if we can avoid it. We have put things in place to protect ourselves. Sometimes that is an order placed in the market; sometimes it means going back to school to learn a missing skill; sometimes it means admitting we are not emotionally ready to trade, for reasons that we have to get straight first.

Lastly, your actual cash balance on deposit with your broker needs to be money that is completely unencumbered for you personally. This needs to be an amount you can emotionally walk away from. Again, this is not as simple as "Only trade with money you can afford to lose." In fact, the exact opposite is a factor that most traders miss until it is too late. If you need those funds for any reason under any potential time frame, you run a risk of cutting your profits short. If you need your starting balance safely back home in, say, six months, suppose you enter a strong position with real potential at the five-month mark? Perhaps that trade might need another four months to develop its full upside potential, and maybe that trade is the big mover in the market this year. Nothing will break a trader's heart faster than having to liquidate a small winner that would have become a huge winner, for the sole reason that those funds are needed for a different purpose and he knew that going in.

Whatever funds you choose to work with, make certain that your risk on those funds includes not needing them later if you can avoid it. If, for instance, you know you will need a certain amount of cash for home repairs in the spring, ask yourself if the money you are depositing in the fall with your broker is intended to be that home repair money. Not only do you risk not getting the repairs done if you have some losses, but if you are on the right side of the big trade for this year, you risk not getting your full benefit if you have to liquidate early for the sake of that pending obligation.

Because there are unlimited ways to lose money once you have placed yourself at risk in a trade, defining your risk incorporates as many of those variables as possible and involves creating as many safety nets as you can. Make this rule work for you by considering the possibility that your personal risk involves something in your life other than your cash trading balance.

Always Place a Protective Stop

I shall tell you a great secret, my friend. Do not wait for the last judgment, it takes place every day.

—Albert Camus

Probably the single most misunderstood rule in the trading game is the rule regarding the use of predetermined exit points, or, as it is commonly stated in the industry, "placing a stop-loss order." Most traders use stop-loss orders ineffectively at best. The most often heard complaint is that liquidating stops are elected right before the market continues farther in the intended direction of the original working trade after only a small correction. Many traders have experienced frustration, anger, or just plain disappointment when a trade that had real potential for gains was stopped out early. However, the issue appears to be more centered on the *proper use* of stop-loss orders, not the question of whether they *should* be used. It only takes one unexpected adverse price move to teach any trader the value of stop-loss orders. It seems everyone wants the protection of stops but genuinely hopes they are never elected.

Without a doubt, there is a tremendous amount of argument and opinion as to what exactly is the best use of stop-loss orders and when trades should be protected. The only part of this debate on which all successful traders agree is that this is the one rule that simply cannot be ignored. Consistently placing and using stop-loss orders on your open positions is your first and best defense against an excessive or unintended loss.

When we first started our discussion of trading rules that work, I made the observation that you cannot consistently trade for profits unless you are on the proper side of the eventual order flow. If you have done your homework and your trade hypothesis turns out to be the correct one for the time in question, the order flow will show up on that side, and until it changes, you are accumulating an open-trade profit. We are concerned with the *net* order flow, not the temporary imbalances that create the ebb and flow of price action on the tick-by-tick basis.

Understanding the net order flow and the potential that the trade may develop is a factor of understanding multiple time frames. I discuss multiple time frames in detail later (see Rule #12), but for the sake of understanding the psychology of using stop-loss orders let's make an assumption: Order flow is *never* perfectly balanced on any one price tick, no matter how many time frames are involved. There will *always* be at least one left-over buy or sell order at every traded price tick. Therefore, the market will always be subject to a temporary imbalance on *some* time frame that will cause prices to flow back and forth many times as that leftover order flow creates the need for the bid or offer to be adjusted.

This knowledge instills the confidence that as long as prices are moving in a general direction over time, we can hold that open position until the full potential develops as we see it. The market might ebb and flow between two price levels for a period of time until it breaks out and reaches our objective, but we can recognize this as "consolidating" or "congestion." The basic price action is not significant enough for us to liquidate the open trade yet; that price action is normal on the way to the eventual objective. We know that markets don't go straight up or straight down; they zigzag back and forth on the way to a particular level—so sitting through that zigzagging action is our goal—except when that supposedly normal zigzag in prices is a full-blown 61.8% retracement covering four weeks of time and 7% of contract price value.

Now we have the issue of placing stops and what to do with them. How do we muster the confidence to hold a position through normal, expected, and healthy price action on the way to our eventual goal? How do we maintain the winning position without getting stopped out on a typical retracement? I think the answer lies in how you define the purpose of stop-loss orders and in understanding what it means to experience the unexpected—which will happen to every trader sooner or later anyway.

I take the point of view that stop-loss orders are not used to protect an open-trade profit. They are not a risk control tool. Stop-loss orders are profit management tools and should not be used to liquidate winning trades. They should be used to liquidate a position—any position—when something has changed with the underlying structure of the market, and not before.

If you follow this thinking to its logical conclusion, that your winning trade is happening only because you are on the right side of the net order flow at that moment, then the best time to liquidate that winning trade will be only at the point when the net order flow in that direction is about over. In other words, you have bought low and sold high for the maximum potential before the net order flow reverses. If you have called it right then the fact is that your protective stop-loss order was never in question—the market had no potential in the direction against you, and you were properly positioned for that order flow. Therefore, the stop was not elected. In fact, you could almost go so far as to say that if the stop order was never placed, the result would have been exactly the same because the *fact* of the order flow was what it was. This is why some people are tempted to trade without stops—but that is a different issue.

MOVABLE STOPS

Why then would you move your stop?

I think that is the critical issue of properly using stop-loss orders. If you have properly identified the net order flow, the stop is not needed and might as well not be there. All the little price ticks in all those tiny little switchbacks or corrections are not the issue; the issue is whether the net order flow has changed. You would only move your stop-loss order if you are not certain that you have identified where the order flow has run out of potential. You place your original stop-loss order only to protect yourself in the event that you have not properly identified the initial place where the order flow will change; if you are incorrect in your entry, you have limited your loss to a predetermined amount according to your system methodology and trade plan.

If you are correct in your assessment, then there is nothing to do but wait until the net order flow runs out of potential in that direction. If you are uncertain of that point, then the movement of the stop closer to the traded prices is your only option. And that brings us to the point of subsequent stop-loss order placement *after* the market has begun to show you an open-trade profit. It is the psychology of moving this stop-loss order that is the central issue of properly using stops, because they are not needed if your first hypothesis is the correct one, unless something has changed and you missed it.

Your only question as it regards moving a stop-loss order closer to the market prices after your winning trade begins working is "What if something changes before I see it change?" There is no other reason to move a stop. At the very least, your trade plan should have some kind of rule that allows you to roll your stop-loss order up to your entry price on open-trade winners, thereby assuming a no-risk trade.

If you intend to use stop-loss orders effectively, you need to use them as a worst-case exit order only. Your first worst-case scenario is being in the market on the wrong side of the order flow at the moment of initial entry. The next-worst case is that the order flow runs out before you have a reasonable lead on the market. The third-worst case is if something changes and you didn't see it coming fast enough to liquidate with what the trade had in it at that point. Otherwise, the only thing to do is wait for your objective.

In my view, rolling stops aggressively to lock in profits is the surest way to cut profits short. Regular ebb and flow in the small order imbalance, regular retracements from significant highs or lows, and random noise between highs and lows are part of the game. It is unlikely that you or any trader will be keen enough on your observation that you will accurately call the near-term price points for such price action. Placing your stops too close to the market is an expression of uncertainty and fear, of attachment to a particular price instead of waiting patiently for the net order flow to run out in that direction. By rolling your stops aggressively you run the risk of having your stops elected by the minor tick-by-tick order imbalance. To avoid this potential, you need to see stops as the method of liquidating only if something has changed. If nothing has changed with the structure of the market, why would you increase your risk by moving a stop-loss order?

One way to make the issue of placing stop-loss orders work for your particular trade approach is to move the stops for only two reasons. The first reason is to take you out at a predetermined dollar loss or gain amount as defined by your risk management rules. In other words, if the trade is working up to a certain amount of open-trade profit, you move your order to secure either a smaller loss/break-even amount or a small profit. After that point, the stop should not be moved until your objective is reached.

The second reason to move a stop would be if you are pyramiding open trade positions. It would be advisable to *always* have a break-even exit stop on your entire position in case something changes and the pyramid begins working against you, and the open trade position falls below your starting equity on the trade.

In all other cases, moving your stops aggressively is a dangerous and unnecessary method of increasing your risk of cutting a profit short. Once a trade has given you a reasonable lead, you can make the near-term assessment that your hypothesis is the correct one. And once that trade is protected for little or no risk, moving a stop-loss order closer to the market on a regular basis will only put you in the position of getting caught in the random minor tick-by-tick action that you have no need to be concerned with anyway. If something has changed, and you don't see it fast enough to keep most of the open-trade profit from evaporating, why would you want to be in a market that you don't see right in the first place?

Always remember that stops are not risk management tools. They are profit management tools. They can only be considered risk management tools if something has changed and you are on the wrong side of the order flow by accident; in which case you would act in your best interest by liquidating anyway—except it happened faster than you could see at your current skill level.

In any case, your equity is protected and you can now look for the next trade with a clear head. Judgment day is every day, so place stops properly.

Your First Loss Is Your Best Loss

Great opportunities come to all, but many do not know they have met them. The only preparation to take advantage of them is simple fidelity to watch what each day brings.

—Albert Dunning

Traders who have a strong personality or high intellectual capacity are often found to be breaking this rule consistently. These traders are often able to call tops and bottoms ahead of major market moves for very concise and accurate reasons. They also tend to execute early on those potential trades and suffer losses before eventually getting on the right side. Their belief in and commitment to their hypothesis is so strong that they continually execute from the side they feel is going to be the big move. Some of these traders have been right in their hypothesis so early and continued to trade from the wrong side for so long that their account has lost significant equity getting to that point. Then when the big move comes, it is really only an opportunity to get back to even.

A bull market can stop being a bull market long before prices top; a bear market can stop being a bear market long before prices bottom. In reality, this is what these traders are usually seeing. They are looking far enough ahead to see a greater potential in the other direction and they know that the turn is coming. They may even spend long hours in analysis looking for that time/price relationship and take quality positions that have an initial small gain; but then the market continues sharply in the original direction and they are taken out. This type of trade situation gives rise to the outdated rule, "Don't pick tops and bottoms," but the fact is that sooner or later a market *must* top or bottom; the lowest risk and highest profit potential are always at the turns.

Identifying those turns is a completely separate issue, and I don't even address it in this book. It is my belief that in today's market climate the tools and knowledge needed to find major turning points are available everywhere. The problem is not in identifying the turns; the problem is being early.

The psychology behind this rule is the issue of nonattachment. Many traders have not developed the underlying ability to adequately detach from price action emotionally. If we have a strong understanding of the market we trade, and we feel very certain in our approach, and we cannot profit unless we buy low and sell high, at some point all of our knowledge and preparation pressures us into an urge for action. We conclude that "the time is now," and we execute. Because we have invested so much of ourselves in forming that conclusion, we have a subconscious attachment to that trade. What we really have is an attachment to that executed price.

When we have formed some kind of attachment to a particular price it is a small step in our thinking that something is "wrong" if prices do not advance favorably in a reasonable amount of time. Having an attachment to pricing is the problem, because prices do not move unless there is order flow on that side. If the price you personally select is not reasonably close to where the order flow is, that trade will simply not work from that particular price at that particular time. It might eventually, and the time for that might be sooner rather than later, but in the meantime nothing is wrong. The market hypothesis that you currently hold might be the exact future that market has in store, but at this particular price/time relationship, you are on the losing side and you simply must stand aside. How you feel about that trade, your knowledge, and your commitment to being in the market have nothing to do with what is actually happening.

By accepting the first loss, you remove yourself from the equation. Notice that I said "accepting the loss." The problem at this moment is *not within the market*. The problem is with the trader and the attachment to the trade hypothesis. The more educated, experienced, or successful any trader becomes, the more susceptible that trader is to trade attachment, especially if he has previously taken a lot of money from that particular market previously.

Developing the ability to remain unattached to your trade results is the issue behind making this rule work for you. No one trader will most likely call a turn in the market at the exact day and time it actually occurs.

Most likely you will be near the price and time that a turn in the market has happened for your time frame and your method. Most likely you will always have slightly more losing trades than winning trades over time. Being emotionally attached or strongly committed to any one price area, any one trade, or one particular side creates an inability to reconsider your hypothesis. Perhaps you are 100% correct about the eventual path that market will take but at this particular moment you are on the losing side of the order flow. Don't argue with it; take a new look at it.

Making this rule work for you is a function of both self-awareness and your methodology. When we create a methodology for trade selection we are attempting to find and exploit an edge in the market. Self-awareness is a completely different part of the trading process, but it is also part of our edge. Only we as individual traders can make the assessment that "the time is now" for our trade approach to be reasonably accurate, and only we as traders can admit it isn't working. The less attachment we have to any one executed trade, the better our net performance will be; our trading methodology will never have 100% winning trades in any case.

Our first loss is our best loss because a loss tells us something very important. A loss tells us that we are on the losing side of the order flow at this moment. That doesn't mean our trade hypothesis is not going to be the correct one at some point; it doesn't mean we as a trader have done something "wrong"; and it doesn't mean we won't be able to make another trade from the same side and have it work at some later time. The only thing you need to accept from a loss is the education it brings. If you as a trader ignore that knowledge, refuse to admit your hypothesis is not an accurate accounting of the market structure, or justify executing again from the same side again without thinking it through, you run the risk of making another loss for the same reason—not knowing the order flow.

Your first loss is your best loss because it opens your information flow to the only two real issues of participating: (1) Get on the right side; (2) if you are on the wrong side, get out. Ignoring, blaming, justifying, getting angry, whatever you feel or do with your first loss does nothing to prevent another loss. The only thing that prevents another loss is finding out what caused this first loss and discovering whether your attachment to your intended result is part of the problem. If you have done a masterful job of pre-trade research and come to a reasonable conclusion that is strong enough for you to commit yourself, you need also to have a reasonable amount of willingness to admit that your hypothesis may be early or incorrect completely. Suppose you are 100% correct but six months early. You could burn through a lot of your trading capital by ignoring the lesson that your first loss could teach you. If your trade hypothesis is completely inaccurate, then you are facing the prospect of a total loss if you ignore the lesson revealed by that first loss.

If you can honestly say to yourself, "I don't care what happens on any one trade," you are a lot closer to getting the real answer to the question "What created the loss?" because the only thing that creates a loss is being on the losing side of the order flow. If you can lay aside all your study, analysis, pain of a cash debit in your account, or emotional frustration, then you most likely can look objectively at the market and find the clues to its actual current structure at that point. Getting on the winning side of the order flow might mean opening another trade from the same side at the same price, or it might not. You might be fairly close to the turn for the next big move, but maybe you won't see it at all if you won't accept the lesson that the first loss is teaching you: "Not yet."

This rule can be a powerful tool for your long-term success. Having a loss for all the right reasons may sound like an oxymoron, but the underlying psychology of this rule carries real benefit to you. A loss simply tells you that you might be early. That is a good problem to have. In the final analysis, you must exercise some kind of foresight to be able to exploit a true inequality in the markets. Having that foresight is something that can be developed. Once you have developed that foresight to some degree, you will also need to develop the ability to time your trades close enough to where the actual change in the order flow is developing. Regardless of how well you personally develop that skill or how you personally create and maintain your edge, you will often be early sometimes. Assume you will have that problem, and take the point of view that your first loss is a megaphone.

Remain completely unattached to the results, seek to understand the order flow, and let your first loss tell you something about how you picked that spot. Don't argue with the market. Listen to what it is saying. Be willing to accept the possibility that your hypothesis is completely inaccurate for the moment.

Never Add to a Loser

If you don't know who you are, the markets are an expensive place to find out.
— George Goodman (paraphrased)

For the most part, almost all losses can be traced back to the same root problem. By *losses*, I don't mean the usual and reasonable winners-versus-losers results that successful traders have; I don't mean "a particular losing trade." In this case I am talking about a consistent and net losing result that occurs over time. The inability to cut losses is the symptom; the actual problem is nearly always a variation of the same basic theme. Most significant or consistent losses are a result of some form of attachment to results on behalf of the trader. Not placing initial stop-loss orders, holding losing trades past a reasonable time, overtrading, and so on are all symptoms of an emotional attachment of some sort. In those cases, the trader simply cannot let go and exit the market. Nothing announces that you have this problem louder than adding to a loser.

This rule, "Never add to a loser," is first cousin to Rule #7. In the case where a trader feels compelled to add to a losing position, the problem is actually a more severe manifestation of attachment. In the case of a loss getting larger than originally intended or several small losses all adding up to a large cash debit, the problem is probably a lack of discipline or a denial of the actual net order flow. In the case of adding to a losing trade the attachment is now a more internal conflict inside the trader and shows a dramatic form of inflexibility.

In this case, a trader is unwilling to see objectively, and the cash loss is ignored while at the same time risk exposure is willingly increased. All other common-sense concerns that at any other time a trader would agree were in the best interest of his account are completely discarded. The trader is actively participating in his own demise. Somewhere inside the trader there is a conflict, and that conflict has nothing to do with market price action or the net order flow. It has to do with the trader's own unwillingness to protect the account, his need to be right, his hope that the market will come back, or any other justification process he might use for holding on to a losing trade in the first place. But instead of simply holding a loser past a certain point, in this case the trader actively increases his risk.

If we stop and use a clear head when we trade, what benefit could we receive by willingly increasing our risk and our cash loss? There is no benefit whatsoever as far as our long-term trading success is concerned. Why then do some traders add to losing positions?

The reasoning behind "Never add to a loser" is very simple: Don't throw good money after bad. The only way you or any trader could be in the position of adding to a losing position is if there was a failure to define the risk before the trade was done in the first place. Rather than accept a reasonable loss and learn the lesson that loss has to teach you the trader, the trader now makes a conscious and deliberate act based not on the fact of the net order flow but on the trader's own emotional need for something. That need may be a need to get back a loss, a need to fight with the market, a need for the market to pay a profit, a need to make a car payment, or any number of little ways of saying the same thing. By adding to a loser, the trader is complicating the process of cutting a loss, thereby making his situation more difficult, but this act is based on something the market has no knowledge of to begin with: *the trader's own emotional need.*

Remember, the market moves only because of the net order flow imbalance. Once you have executed and are now in a position, you are no longer in control of the net result to your equity. If you are not on the correct side of the net order-flow as far as your chosen position is concerned, your account will accrue a cash debit until either you liquidate or the net order flow turns in your favor. If the net order-flow never turns in your favor it is possible you could run out of margin funds before the price action stabilizes. By doing anything other than liquidating, you are increasing the risk that you will suffer ruin. Adding to a losing position is actually *pyramiding* your loss! As an intelligent individual, how ridiculous does this sound to you? What trader would willingly put himself in the poorhouse at a geometrically faster rate?

As a serious trader looking to master your game, you cannot afford to allow emotional or perceived psychological needs to influence your willingness to protect yourself. The reason you must never add to a loser under any circumstances is because the probability of being on the correct side of the order flow has *already* become evident due to the open-trade loss you are already holding. You are on the losing side to begin with; you haven't seen it right, and that *fact* alone, in and of itself says "liquidate"—nothing else. Failure to liquidate means a bigger loss. Adding to the loser means an even *bigger* loss. How is that in your best interest?

Ask yourself exactly why you feel the desire to add to an existing loss. If you take a step back and think it through, the reason will most likely be some form of emotional attachment to the trade results and some form of unwillingness to do the right thing. Adding to a loser is a symptom of a bigger problem the trader has: no real control over his feelings or emotions. A trader in that position is an accident waiting to happen.

Some traders make the mistake of defining a losing trade as a function of cash debit. By that I mean, an entry execution is followed by a liquidation execution and the two prices marked into the trading account yield a net negative dollar amount. I think it is far more beneficial for you to redefine the concept of a loss to include more focus on the issue of personal discipline.

If you find yourself executing into a market for some reason and, on further evaluation of your actions, you come to the conclusion that you are doing the wrong thing for you personally, then you need to liquidate to exit the market immediately. If you have broken a trading rule, if you have done a trade because of something you normally wouldn't trust as an indicator, if you have emotionally wanted a profit, or whatever other misstep you may have made, you are most likely taking more risk than you otherwise would have. Ruthlessly liquidating to protect yourself is your best option, *even if the trade has an open-trade profit at that point.* A losing trade can be any trade done for any reason if your personal discipline has been broken in order to make that trade.

Once you redefine a losing trade from the standpoint of your personal discipline and not as a change in your cash balance, you are in a position to learn what you need to learn from your first loss—how to effectively participate on the right side. The issue of adding to a loser is never in question because you aren't trading from a financial focus to begin with. You are trading from the focus of discipline to do the proper thing *all the time.* You will not be tempted to add to your loser because you will have cut the loss by liquidating. You can always get back in, so there is no need to hold something that isn't working and certainly no need to make matters worse by adding to something that isn't working.

Fundamentally, making this rule work means admitting to yourself that you need something to control your emotional bias as it creates your urge to action. You need to confront the possibility that you personally have a "something" somewhere in your thinking and recognize that that particular little something has nothing to do with successful trading. The next time that particular little something shows up for trading, you will have already decided that you are not going to break your discipline today. The urge to add to a loser is a signal to liquidate because *something is not right with me today*. If something is not right with you, the trader, that has nothing to do with market structure or where the net order flow is. If you aren't seeing it correctly today, that is clearly shown by an open-trade loss to begin with. At that point you liquidate.

Making Rule #7 work will lead to never breaking Rule #8. The only difference between the two is the trader's depth of attachment to the trade.

Don't
Overtrade

*I will say this again, I never made my money by
trading; I made my money by sitting tight.*
                                        —Jesse Livermore

Overtrading is the definitive symptom of the net losing trader. All the
other errors that can increase the net outflow of trading capital
from a trading account can be found when you examine the
amount of executions done overtime. Could you say that adding to a losing trade is overtrading? Isn't it true that too many trades are often done
by failing to define a risk?

As I mentioned in the Introduction, most of the trading rules we are
familiar with need to be examined from the perspective of the psychology
either helping us develop or preventing us from developing. Many people
arrive at Rule #9, "Don't overtrade," as a wake-up call only after it is too
late. To make this rule work we need to understand that it is a guideline
that will help us prevent blowing ourselves out of the water. In reality,
overtrading can be many things, but one thing is certain: Ignoring the potential we have to overtrade will almost surely put us in the position where
we have overtraded—and by the time we wake up to this fact, our equity
is gone.

Part of the problem we as traders seem to have is processing the voluminous amount of market information and opportunity base that is available to us. At this critical point in monetary evolution, the financial
markets are exponentially growing in both size and complexity. In addition
to the explosive growth across virtually all sectors of money management

services, the evolution of communication is also growing at a phenomenal rate. At the time of this writing, any individual with reasonable means located in a developed area has instant access to almost any other individual, source of information, or market center anywhere in the world instantaneously via the Internet, cell phone, or television. I live and work in downtown Chicago, but if I wanted to I could have complete access to everything I have now from a sailboat in the Caribbean or a mountaintop in India; and so could you. As traders we are no longer limited by distance or connectivity to any market or information base. If we perceive that an opportunity exists in an area somewhere on the other side of the world from our home, we can choose from an almost unlimited number of ways to exploit that opportunity and an equally unlimited information flow to manage that opportunity.

A key to cutting our losses is selecting which opportunities are the best profit potential for us personally and if the truth were told, we really need only one market. The fact that we can actively participate globally at any moment contributes at least in part to the problem of overtrading.

Many traders make the mistake of thinking that the term *overtrading* can only mean excessive trading in a particular market. Although that is one aspect of it and needs to be addressed as part of your loss-control strategy, it would be far more accurate to rephrase this rule as "Don't overcommit." It really doesn't matter precisely what that means for you directly, but as a serious student of lasting trade success, you must make choices about how to allocate your limited resources. No one has unlimited capital and no one has unlimited mental or emotional resources. Yes, you must have controls on your behavior to prevent excessive trading within one market, but you must also narrow your focus down to a specific number of markets and the reasons you trade them. It is unreasonable to think you will perform equally well in all markets across all opportunities.

Without a solid understanding of each particular market and how each is structured, you will run the risk of having losses you cannot explain to yourself. Worse yet, because you cannot easily find the cause of your lack of profitability in one particular market, you will most likely continue to have losses in that market. Many traders have complained of net losing years or flat years while showing closed profits in one market against closed losses in another. The common complaint goes something like, "If only I hadn't traded in crude oil! I made six figures in the S&Ps!"

Learning to stop overtrading requires a willingness to limit your opportunity base while simultaneously maximizing your effectiveness in the markets you will trade. It does no long-term good for your trading account to have significant gains in one market offset by losses in another. Additionally, overtrading is a symptom of a trader's impatience with the opportunity he has selected or frustration over the results he has achieved. No long-term successful trader ever complains about opportunity or how long it takes to develop. Such a trader has learned that certain times are better for executing than others, and that no matter what, it will take some amount of time to see results. If nothing is happening today, then nothing is happening today. The market that trader is working in simply doesn't have a lot to offer at this particular time. The wise trader is not concerned with that issue because he knows how to trade that market and he doesn't have his focus degraded by trying to put effort into seven different places which he can't exploit as effectively as he can one.

Because we as traders have so many choices and so much information available to us, we are tempted to think all *perceived* opportunities will remain *actual* opportunities for us personally, simply because we have access to something we ordinarily may have never known about before. We think that access to information is a de facto source of opportunity, when in reality our own ability to manage opportunity and information flow is the real key to our long-term success. One aspect of making the rule "Don't overtrade" work for you directly is to narrow your focus to the best possible market opportunities for you personally and limit your information flow to only the critical information needed to exploit that number of market opportunities.

As an example, if you cannot understand why China is the fourth-largest economy in the world today but won't revalue their currency to reduce their trade surplus, then buying a China-based mutual fund for your long-term IRA stock account may not be a good move, even though that fund meets your basic criteria for risk/reward ratio and has four confirming technical indicators that you have come to trust well. Letting that trade go because you don't have time to understand global economics well enough to know when it will be time to liquidate that trade might save you a significant amount of capital should you miss something along the way. The fact that you can follow the Hang Sang index in real time and get English-translation market commentary twice a day from Hong Kong does not mean you will be able to put it together well enough to effectively trade that opportunity from your home in the United States. It is tempting to think you can, but you might be overtrading your limited resources if you can't. A 40% loss in something you don't understand rips the bottom out of two solid years in a "beat the S&P 500" trade you found. I am not saying it is a bad idea to consider globalizing your opportunity base. I am saying it is a bad idea to spread yourself too thin just because you can.

The common understanding of the rule "don't overtrade" is related to multiple executions within an existing market you currently trade in. This rule is designed to prevent you from exposing yourself to excessive low-probability trades. The most common symptom of breaking this rule is executing multiple times from roughly the same area on the same side, but also taking multiple losses. Basically, you make six or seven trades from the long side, for example, and have five individual losses and a net loss on the day. To make matters worse, if you would have just sat tight on the first position for the whole day, you would have had a nice gain by the close.

Overtrading (as defined by multiple executions) is a function of not understanding your time frame properly, not following your rules to begin with, or not following your trade system properly. When the trader chooses to do something he ordinarily wouldn't do, he is showing his emotional attachment to his results instead of maintaining a focused behavior congruent with his discipline. Overtrading is a symptom of attachment, as is all consistently losing trading behavior.

To make this rule work for you, create a baseline of behavior that is consistent with your trading system and your trading plan. It really doesn't matter what that baseline is initially, but you have to create it as an independent set of behavior controls, separate from your trading system or plan. For example, if you are using an execution system that makes a trade call about once a day, and you are using that system properly, it would be rare for you to have four executions to initiate in a single day in a single market. If you find you are executing more aggressively than the system actually tells you to, then you are overtrading. It is not a subjective or emotional set of data; it is a factual set of results that says, "You are not following the rules today." It doesn't matter if your system is a moving average crossover signal with a 15-minute moving average convergence divergence (MACD) confirmation; if you aren't following it, you actually have no system. And it doesn't matter if your trade plan calls for you to take a break after two consecutive winning weeks and take your family to dinner with some of your profits; you aren't going to have any profits.

The symptom of overtrading is often subtle so that by the time you are willing to admit you are doing it, the damage is done. Therefore, to make this rule work you have to choose ahead of time to put controls on your behavior *before* you overtrade. You must write yourself a few rules that lead to *preventing* overtrading, not helping you recover after you have done the damage. That rule set is unique to you—it is a factor of your particular systemized approach and what it would look like if you weren't following it.

The key to making this rule work for you is to ask yourself what it would look like if you were actually overtrading, based on the unique probabilities inherent in your trade system being compromised. Once you have that data, you must create a rule that would prevent that happening, *if you follow it*. In many cases, traders do not really know what their trade system probabilities are and therefore can't really get the data to know what overtrading would look like. Overtrading is not as simple as "trading too much." If your system has a 55% probability of a winner but gets two-thirds of those trades on a Monday, you would be overtrading if you did a large number of trades on a Friday; so for you and your system, the definition of *overtrading* is not necessarily relative to the total trades created by that system. In this case, the rule "Don't overtrade" might mean not trading more than twice on a Friday, but that wouldn't apply on Monday. Maybe Monday's rule would be "Don't trade more than eight times."

Gathering the data to exploit your system's inherent probabilities is one thing, but putting controls on your behavior when you are outside those parameters depends on your knowing the difference. In any case, your trading plan is worthless if your systemized approach is not being followed properly. The rule "Don't overtrade" is a call for you to get good data and then implement it into your trading plan. That includes both knowing which opportunities to trade in the first place, and being willing to admit that you may be not be exploiting those opportunities as well as you could. Both sides of the overtrading issue are about reducing risk exposure until you have the data to make a significant improvement to your market presence. The goal, of course, is to gather both the data and the will to follow your rules before burning through all your capital.

Following Rule #9 can boil down to answering this question as honestly as you can:

"How well do I know what I am doing, and am I willing to admit I don't?" If the answer to that question is anything other than "I know exactly and I don't need to change anything," you are most likely overtrading in some form or another. You are either trading too many markets for you, trading without knowing your exact probabilities, or doing a little of both. Reducing your exposure or knowing when to stop executing (or a little of both) depends on your willingness to control yourself. Unwillingness to control your behavior is what leads to breaking every other rule. Overtrading is the most important symptom to look for. We find out how bad we have the problem next in Part III, "Letting Profits Run."

Letting Profits Run

Keep Good Records and Review Them

Mistakes are a fact of life: It is the response to the error that counts.
—Nikki Giovanni, *Forbes Thoughts on Opportunity*

Many traders experience an initial level of success easily right at the start of their trading. They open their first account and begin trading, maybe with a very simple approach, and with only a handful of trades they earn a substantial gain in a short period of time. Naturally, it would be easy for the trader to make the assumption, "This is easy!"

Of course you know the rest of the story. Over time this particular trader loses his initial winnings and then proceeds to lose some or all of his initial balance just as quickly. Some traders repeat this process over and over again with a new trading stake and a new system. It is very tempting to think the problem was the system used the first time, or maybe the amount of capital wasn't big enough to take advantage of the system's full potential and probabilities. It is very easy for people to make the erroneous assumption that they know what they are doing only because they have a little early success at something.

Very few traders want to admit that much of their beginning success is due completely to luck. But the fact of the matter is if you *did* know what you were doing or had *really* found the perfect system, you would have a consistent positive result no matter what the market conditions are. Some people are better at this game than others, and their success is the result of a programmed and proactive methodology involving every possible advantage a trader can find that can be applied with flawless discipline.

To accumulate consistent and significant profitability requires doing some things that at first may not seem valuable. But true professional traders will tell you that getting to the point of solid success that can be consistently duplicated in any market requires perfect application of skill and knowledge.

So where do you get the knowledge and how do you acquire the skill?

In this part of the book, we are discussing the rules for letting profits run. Most traders feel that a proper discussion of letting profits run would be market-related and include lots of details on stop-loss placement, adding to open positions, expanding time frames, and so forth. But in my view, the most significant part of getting more money out of your winning trades is to know *exactly* how you created them and then duplicate that success more often. If you do not know *exactly* how you created a winning trade and then know *exactly* how you can duplicate that winning behavior again and again, your gains are at best limited or, at worst, completely due to luck. You must know what you are doing right and what you can improve. This is more than a vague agreement you have with yourself; this is a matter of getting data. The pathway to more consistent profits is record keeping.

Why record keeping?

Think of a book that you were required to read during your college years. No matter what your initial response to your course load or even your particular interest in your course work, you were not going to pass any course unless you absorbed the material required by your teacher and could demonstrate to his satisfaction that you had that knowledge inside your head. You were required to read that book, make critical distinctions about the point the author was trying to make, and then you would be given a test; and if you failed the test you got no credit for the course. That is a fact.

In the world of the markets the process is really not materially different. You need certain knowledge and if you can't pass the test (trade successfully), you get no credit for the course (you don't make any money). To make things a bit more complicated, you have probably guessed that there is a book or two you will need to read to acquire the knowledge you need to pass the test. The twist is that *you* write the book you need to read.

Record keeping is your most important asset in your quest to master the skill of letting profits run. By compiling a complete and accurate written record of your personal trade approach, an accurate accounting of your mental and emotional state, and the actual record of how well you are following your trade system and your trade plan, you create a huge database of information you can now use to *learn from your own actions* what you are doing that works and what you are doing that needs to be improved or even eliminated from your behavior. By critically reviewing things like your records of execution for entry and exit, when you made a change in your position, trades you didn't take, your notes about your thinking, and so on, you have the hard data required for you to ascertain what you were doing and what you were not doing. Your records are a *factual accounting of what happened*, leading to the results you now have. You can see by study exactly *how* you created a winner or loser at a particular date and time. You can see similarities and inadequacies. You can understand parts of your actions and how easy it might be to change some behavior that usually leads to a loss or cuts a profit short. In short, you have the data you need to critically examine in order to pass the test required to receive credit for the class—to pull the most money out of the market.

The true and lasting benefit of accurate record keeping is the ability to observe *from the outside* your behavior as it *actually is* when you trade. As you compile more and more data about your *actual* behavior and see clearly how that differs from your *desired* behavior, you create a source of information that can assist you in *modifying* your behavior. In the final analysis, your *actual behavior* is what creates your actual results. If you are willing to admit that it is your behavior that creates a larger loss, cuts a profit short, hesitates at the best entry or exit point, then you have a choice to modify your behavior and increase your probability of success. You have the ability to see clearly *where* in your behavior you are doing things that lead to losses and *where* in your behavior you are cutting your winners short. After that point you can now create rules to modify your behavior and those rules are the same ones we discuss here, with one important distinction: You now know where the problem is *for you personally* and you now know you can *fix* it.

In my view, accurate record keeping is not as simple as "writing everything down." I think you will achieve more lasting success as a trader if you know what you need to keep records of and exactly what you are looking for inside that data. Gathering hard data in the arena of trading is both an inner and outer process. You need to accurately record all of your outer behavior, which includes execution entry, stop placement, moving stops, setting limits, adding to positions, taking off positions, final liquidation, when stops/limits were filled, dates and times of all these actions, and the net gain or loss to your account.

Inner data is far more valuable and difficult to document, but the inner data is the real meat and potatoes of getting better at trading. Remember, no matter how you want to slice it, you *must* be on the proper side of the *net* order flow reasonably close to your entry point in order to at the very least have an open-trade profit working for you. If anything is getting in the way of your seeing the most probable point where the net order flow is likely to change, your probabilities of success on that trade are lower.

One thing you must do in the record-keeping process is to document *exactly* what you are thinking and feeling when you execute. Keep a written journal of your thoughts and emotions. The sole purpose of this documentation is to expose to your conscious mind the true nature of what you are using from your inner world when you execute, move orders, take yourself out of trades, or refrain from taking trades. All of your thoughts, perceptions, feelings, desires, motivations, and so on boil around inside your internal trade-making software and finally create an urge to action— the reason *why* you pull the trigger at that precise spot.

The sum total of your inner world is what creates your account balance for the simple reason that you see the market the way *you* see it. Your systematic trading approach is an attempt to create a sense of order to understand the apparent chaos of price action. It is designed to help you find the best possible point for a change in the net order flow, based on some hypothesis of probabilities that you hope are usually present under certain time frames. What your system really does for you is give you enough confidence to execute. It gives you that confidence because the systematic approach is based on a set of assumptions that you can agree with ahead of time. All you need to do is follow the system—but market conditions and your personal state of mind may not be exactly right for that system today.

When you make the choice to trade or not trade for some reason, you create only one of three results: made money, lost money, or stood aside. No matter the results in your trading account, there was movement in the market anyway. If you see that movement as a potential profit you missed, a potential loss you avoided, a trade you shouldn't have done, or a trade that was done right, you are no longer trading the system. You are trading your *point of view* on the results of using or not using the system. The market itself had no knowledge of your participation or absence, and your results had nothing to do with the net order flow.

This inner data is invaluable to know about yourself because it will expose your thinking process for what it is at the time. After critically examining your thoughts and emotions, comparing them to the financial results in your account, and then finally to subsequent price action, you will see how *fear, greed,* or *hope* was involved in your execution instead of *clarity of observation* or *discipline*. Once that is clear to you, the choice to change both your thinking and your behavior is yours. If you know that when certain things are going through your mind you are about to either make a losing trade or get out of a winner too soon, you can make the choice to stay out or hold on a bit longer. Your confidence is better because you control your behavior better.

Record keeping on both levels will give you that extra data to learn where you are strong and where you are weak in your trading approach. After critically examining your own documented behavior you can see where you excel in trading, and you can then duplicate that winning behavior. You will also see where your behavior is weak, and you can put controls (rules) in place to minimize their effect on your execution. In the end, it is only your behavior that creates your results. You need to know what behavior works and what behavior doesn't, and in most cases that data is in your head when you trade. Get that data out on the table and study it.

In the Introduction I briefly discussed one change I made to my trading approach after I started to keep good records and review them. I learned to stay out of the market when I personally needed to and to trust my analysis. Making that one change put me on the right side of the net order flow better, which allowed me to hold my winners for the best potential. Yet when I reviewed the records after that point, I discovered that my total trade results where not materially different; I had about the same number of winners and losers and made about the same number of trades in a quarter. Most of my net gain was from only a handful of the trades—the ones I was holding. I plotted this data using a standard bell curve and plotted my previous results on top of that. I discovered that from a pure probability standpoint, nothing had changed. So why was my account balance higher?

My account balance was higher because I held my winning trades and made fewer total trades *before* the winning trades. Prior to the new rule I enforced on my behavior, the overtrading yielded small gains and losses, and that kept my balance orbiting around a basic area of pre-winner loss. By not having those losses to overcome, when I would hold the winner for the pull, instead of overcoming a loss prior I was adding a profit prior. It is similar to positive cash flow as opposed to negative—like getting paid, paying all your bills, and having nothing left, versus paying all your bills, getting paid, and having no obligations. My account balance went higher, slightly lower, higher, slightly lower, instead of going lower, slightly higher, lower, slightly higher, yet the actual trading was about the same. I really didn't do anything different in my analysis or trade selection; I just got positioned better by *knowing* where I was weak and knowing where I was strong. My record keeping showed me that, and if I hadn't kept those records I may have not learned that as quickly or had the data to make that small change.

Add to
Your Winners

He that would have fruit must climb the tree.
—Thomas Fuller

No one can successfully speculate to their full potential until they have the capacity to consistently add to winning positions. I make this statement for three reasons. First of all, the pure probabilities of any systemized trading approach will always be subject to a ratio of winning trades to losing trades. If, for whatever reason, the winning trades are not maximized to their full potential then your net results over time will usually never be more than average across the entire sample set.

I would encourage you to do a little homework on various systems and their net results over time. You will discover that almost all systems (no matter how they were developed or the theory behind them) suffer a period of drawdown that reduces their overall net results. If the user of a given system has used it for any reasonable amount of time prior to the drawdown point, no matter the previous success earned, the results are usually no better than a small gain or loss. If the user of that system has only used it a short time prior to a drawdown, then the results are usually negative to the account equity. This, of course, does not take into account the actual trader executing and how well he follows the system to begin with. Many winning systemized approaches are negated by the behavior of the trader using it.

Second, market quality is never discussed in system methodology. All back-testing is based on the "if–then" assumption that conditions in any market will be basically identical in time forward as they were in time past. In other words, the system is supposed to create results, from the point it is actually used in a real trading market, similar to those it generated as it hypothetically performed in markets that had already been traded. But the underlying conditions of that back-tested market cannot be duplicated forward, and the system methodology cannot account for underlying conditions as they may change. Therefore, the established probabilities learned from the system's methods may not be duplicated if underlying conditions are creating price action that the system has never been exposed to before. The system's win/loss ratio might be higher or lower and the money taken from winners may not be enough to overcome the money lost on the losers.

Part of the reason that systems have drawdowns to begin with is because the system is being overlaid onto a market that has a different underlying condition than the one that the system methodology was developed under. The perfect example is a trend-following approach being overlaid onto a market that has stopped trending due to a change in the underlying fundamentals and/or the perception of traders. The win/loss ratio will most likely drop and the losing trades will most likely be larger than the winning trades. Adding to the winners in this case becomes more critical if you intend to keep using that system while you wait for the resumption of trend.

Third, adding to winners is the best method of letting profits run for the simple reason that the net order flow in the direction of your trade may continue for quite some time past your initial best estimate. When we discuss using multiple time frames (Rule #12) and buying and selling 50% retracements (Rule #25), you will have more tools for adding to your winners because often the depth of the net order flow can develop over time, and it may not be apparent until you have been in the trade for a while. Sometimes the quality of the market changes in your favor to a deeper and more definable way *after* you have executed to take your initial position. Being alert and ready for this eventuality is the psychology behind Rule #11, "Add to your winners."

Adding to your winners does not necessarily refer to a particular price point. It is often a *price/time relationship*. For example, suppose you have established a particular market position for a period of time and it currently has an open-trade profit, but the market itself has started to consolidate between two very well-defined price areas. Having done your homework, you already know that this particular market is subject to consolidation when waiting for a particular set of fundamentals to develop. You already know that conditions are bullish and you are waiting for that consolidation to break out to the upside, but that would mean a new monthly high for that market. The fundamentals are due at the end of the month, and prior to that point the volume has been dropping daily, but the market is remaining well bid during this time.

If the market breaks out to the upside, you want to add to your open longs because a new monthly high will attract a lot of attention from people who may be waiting for some sort of confirmation before committing themselves to a long position. As the time approaches for the new set of closely watched fundamentals to be released, you notice that the market firms near the top of the range and volume is increasing a bit. Now the news is released and the market breaks out to the upside and never looks back. That would indicate that a potentially new net order flow is coming in, and even though prices are now at your first objective on your first long, the better thing to do is hold that trade and add to it because *now* the long position has *more* potential than you first anticipated—and you are already there with a lead.

Of course, if the opposite had happened, you would also know that the potential in the long position is dropping and you might want to liquidate; but that is another issue. In the case of an upside breakout at a significant price/time relationship, you have a new clue that something is changing, and that very well could mean more potential in the direction you had originally participated in. You need to press your advantage and not only hold that winner but consider adding to the open trade for a maximum gain. A system cannot account for that potential; only *you* can.

On a *close and reverse* strategy the same thinking applies. If you are aggressive in one direction and something changes—not only liquidating your open trade but reversing completely and holding a new trade in the other direction, if that price action is more aggressive and maybe even breaks back through your original price from the first trade's entry—you are in a position where you could very well have tapped into a very large new net order flow and you are apparently on the right side. You need to consider adding to the second working trade. Some old trading rules actually are based on this thinking, one of which is "Buy/sell a reversal back through the opening range." In today's 24-hour marketplace this rule is obsolete in many markets, but the psychology is the same: Add to your winner when the net order flow is very clear to be expanding in your direction.

The key here is not to say you will *always* add to your winners but that you will always be *ready to* add to your winners when the net order flow is clearly apparent to you and you already have a lead on the market. In other words, when you are seeing it clearly and you are being paid, ask the market to pay you more since it apparently wants to.

A key to making this rule work consistently for you is to develop the mind-set that market conditions are dynamic. They are constantly changing. When they change in your favor you need to exploit that, especially when you are already in the market holding a winner. Adding to a winner is really not a factor of increasing your risk. Your risk is always identical all the time: "What if I am on the wrong side of the net order flow?" The fact that market conditions can and will change is not the issue. The issue is getting paid the most when they change and losing the least when they change.

When conditions are not changing and a trade is working, at some point you want to add to that winner to maximize your profits. You would liquidate that trade at your objective anyway, regardless of whether you had one contract working or a hundred. After you add to that winner, if something changes against you, either you would take your position off or be stopped out—again, regardless of whether you had one contract on or a hundred. However you decide that the rule set for adding to a winner is going to work for you, the strategy is less important than *always being ready to use it*. If conditions change for the better in your favor, the issue of adding to a winner should never be in question. Press the advantage that you already have.

Think of this rule as *proactive*. You are taking control of your ultimate trading success by choosing to place yourself in the best possible profit. You are choosing to take what is there to get. Remember, this rule will not work well for you if you add to winners *hoping* the market will continue in your favor. You need to be certain you have identified the remaining potential in the trade. *Proactively* choosing to say, "As long as conditions remain as they are, I will take more out," needs to be effectively balanced against "If conditions change, *I am out*." There can be no other influence on your adding to a position. You add when your level of certainty is highest in your original trade hypothesis. As long as your hypothesis remains the correct one, you stay in that trade until your objective is reached or something changes.

Sometimes adding to a winner is a factor of conditions remaining the same until you reach the objective. Sometimes adding to that winner is a factor of conditions unexpectedly improving in your direction. But in any case, when you are on the correct side of the net order flow, once that is solidly confirmed to you, no matter how you choose to define it or what tools you use to confirm it, adding to that winner is your best option to maximize your profitability and negate the opposing probabilities inherent in any systemized trading approach. Your systemized approach will have weak spots and a drawdown can happen at any time. Remaining vigilant and prepared to add to a winner will help increase your chance of lasting success. Part of your trading plan should include a regular assessment of how well you are applying this rule.

One consideration that will help you identify when it is time to add to an open-trade winner is a rise in *volume* on days the market is moving in the intended direction. If that is accompanied by a rise in *open interest*, so much the better, but you need to see *turnover* at times when the market is advancing in your direction. Remember when we briefly discussed the issue of zero-sum transactions? The only trader who *must* execute is the one holding the losing position; he has to get out at some point because he cannot lose money forever. When that losing position is liquidated, at least one contract is not there anymore, so open interest will drop. If this losing trader reenters the market and then experiences another loss, volume will be higher but the net open interest should still reflect his leaving the market. In other words, the same trader did one lot for a net loss on the day, but he did it four times. Therefore, volume is higher but open interest is around the same for the day because he is not holding overnight.

Turnover on days when price action is net in the direction of your hypothesis usually means the same groups of losers are coming back and the same groups of winners are taking their money. This situation gets better if *new* winners and *new* losers are squaring off; a rise in open interest will result. In this case, because the price action is still net in one direction, it is evident that the sum total of the orders from that side remains higher than the other side, no matter who is winning or losing *net on the day*. The market will continue in that direction until everybody quits, which is shown by a drop in open interest. That usually signals you are near a turn. Watching for turnover is a great clue that it is time to add to your open-trade winner. If that is accompanied by a rise in open interest, you know the market has a lot of fuel left in it, so you can continue to add.

Maybe you could add every day for weeks and take it all . . .

Use Multiple Time Frames

Think fast—act slow.
—Greek proverb

Most traders have had the frustrating experience of having a nice winning trade suddenly reverse into a smaller gain or, worse yet, a loss, execute for their liquidation, and then watch that trade run in their favor to a new daily or weekly profit level. Aside from placing their stop too close (or panicking out), this problem is a result of not understanding multiple time frames and how groups of traders on different time frames compete with one another for control of the market. If you look at your historical price charts, you will observe that retracements, false breakouts, reversals, failed reversals, washouts, and various other price patterns occur with regular frequency under all time frames. A short-time-frame price chart and a long-time-frame price chart will eventually have the same or similar patterns develop; the only difference is *actual* time required to create that price pattern or see that potential developing—"clock time," if you will.

I find it is more helpful to think of price charts not in terms of a time frame per se but more as a *number of bars*. For example, a typical pennant formation requires around 40 to 60 bars of "open-high-low-close" (OHLC) price bars to form and be observed as a potential pennant. On a five-minute price chart, that would represent about 200 to 300 minutes of clock time—somewhere around 3.3 to 5.0 hours by the clock. If you have done your homework, you know that a pennant formation has a certain probability of a breakout at a certain time (about two-thirds of the way forward from the mast or flagpole) and that the price move is usually about the distance of the flat side of the pennant, one way or the other.

In other words, on a five-minute price chart, if you suspect a pennant is forming, it will take you about two to three hours to define it, and somewhere around the four-hour mark a breakout higher or lower is a higher probability. Additionally, most pennants on a five-minute price chart have a flat side of some amount that is a certain percent of the day's range. Armed with this data you now enter that trade, and if all goes smoothly, you might capture 80% or more of the breakout when it comes. But at that moment, a new level of order flow comes in and that market really takes off. And identifying that new net order flow is what makes all the difference.

Using that hypothetical trade as an illustration, if you compare your five-minute price chart to an hourly time frame price chart, perhaps you will then observe a different pattern that the last 40 to 60 bars have created. Upon closer examination you note that the pennant formation that required 60 bars and 300 minutes by the clock is reflected on the hourly price chart as a *double-top* formation that required 6 bars and 300 minutes by the clock. If your five-minute pennant formation had an upside breakout, once your price objective was reached, that most likely was near the top of the hourly double-top formation. Should the market now attract enough buying to penetrate the hourly double-top, you would be out of the trade with a small profit just when the larger-time-frame trader is buying into the market and creating a bigger order imbalance on the buy side. You have banked a small profit when you could have just as easily had a larger one by simply noting that the smaller-time-frame bullish potential was contained within a larger-time-frame bullish potential. Both time frames had a bullish potential that developed within the same 300 minutes by the clock, even though each price chart counted it differently and presented that data to the observer (you) in two different formats.

The concept of using multiple time frames has to do with understanding who is looking at what, and when those traders are most likely to add pressure to the order flow by entering an order. An hourly-based trader is thinking something different, and therefore executing differently, than someone on a longer or shorter time frame. When you have a lot of evidence on your side, in your time frame, that it is time to enter the market from one particular side, how confident are you that more orders from a different time frame will also be coming in from that side? You can develop that confidence by seeing objectively what other time frames are seeing. When you then compare those viewpoints for congruency, if you have a good sense that more than one time frame is thinking along the same lines, you have more confirmation that potential net order flow may develop a little larger along that direction. To help you let your profits run, you need to recognize and exploit what *every* time frame might eventually be doing.

Your best trades occur when you have correctly positioned yourself on the net order flow as traders in each successively higher time frame choose to execute. For example, if you are looking for a buy point, you would like to see the 5-minute, 10-minute, and 15-minute price charts provide similar clues, all at around the same price area. At the exact same time, the 30-minute and hourly price charts are likely neutral or slightly bearish after a move to the downside has already happened. The daily and weekly price charts might show a down day or weekly low within a broader weekly or monthly established range.

Now, suppose you execute from the buy side and within 30 minutes or so you have an open-trade profit. Most likely you have correctly identified where the 30-minute-or-less trader is creating a buy-side order imbalance because prices are higher. That can't happen unless sellers are overwhelmed under those conditions at that moment. If the 30-minute and hourly bars now trade higher, then you have a pretty good clue that traders in the next higher time frame are also beginning to show up *on the buy side.* If the market now continues higher and closes, say, in the upper half of the daily range, it is a fairly good bet that the daily-time-frame buyer is also executing. If the market is again higher for the next day's trading by the close, the traders looking for a potential low for the week may be active from the buy side. Your original entry on the shorter time frame is *confirmed* by the longer-time-frame traders executing from the same side. More traders are seeing the same thing, and the cumulative net order flow is working from that side. In this illustration, competing time frames became congruent as the market drew in the full spectrum of participants the more clock time passed. As time goes on, the market will continue to advance even when the short-term time frame produces a sell signal because the larger time frame is still attracting order flow from the buy side.

Now, bear in mind, I am not trying to oversimplify price action or getting positioned. I know that swings in price can be violent, the market might go sideways for a long time, and false signals frequently occur all the time. Often trades that could have worked become losers for various reasons. It takes time to get in a position, and it takes experience to know when the move you are waiting for is developing.

The point I want you to absorb is that certain trades from one side *develop potential over time.* Sometimes closing out your position with a good gain because it was one of the biggest moves you had ever seen under your time frame is the worst thing you can do. If the larger-time-frame traders are drawn in from the same side, that particular market will have a lot farther to go in your original direction. Of course, you can always get back in from the original side anytime you want, and maybe it is a good rule for you personally to remain flat overnight; but if you are following this rule properly you will always look for clues that the winning position you just found and participated in has a lot more potential developing in the same direction.

It takes *clock time* for all those trading time frames to become active. If traders in multiple time frames are coming into the market, your probability of success is much better. When this rule is combined with Rule #11, you have a powerful tool to help you let profits run better. When a position has worked, consider that if it is still working a day or two later, you might want to look at that side again and also add to it.

Making this rule work for you requires you to think outside the box as it concerns your personal time frame. You should always have a time frame that you execute under, but that time frame does not contain all the information about potential net order flow. The wise trader will consider what the traders with other time frames might be seeing, because at some point, when those other time frames are drawn in, their orders from those different time frames will either add to the net order flow that is developing in one direction or it will overwhelm the net order flow from the other side, stopping the imbalance and the price advance. Every trader who has the potential to execute will affect the net order flow. Whether those traders are using a larger or smaller time frame than you is not important. What is important is whether the potential they offer will be for or against the net order flow currently operating in the market. In other words, if they come in with their potential, will that potential increase the imbalance or reduce it?

By observing price patterns in several time frames, you can begin to see which direction the market is more likely to go. By using more than one time frame to evaluate a trade's potential, you will avoid more low-probability trades. When several time frames are all saying about the same thing and prices are advancing in that direction, as clock time passes, that trade's potential is increasing. If several time frames appear to offer conflicting price pattern relationships, that trade most likely has a lower potential. As a trader looking for high-probability trades, develop the skill of comparing multiple time frames to your trade hypothesis. When you have a good idea that traders in the next few higher time frames are interested in the same side as you are, you need to let them have the clock time they need to execute.

Also, be prepared for your time frame to give a liquidation signal when the higher time frames are getting their initiation signal. A key to holding your winners and using multiple time frames is learning that a shorter time frame *needs* to offer a countertrend signal to encourage the trader from the opposite side to initiate. That opposite-side order from the shorter-time-frame trader is what the higher-time-frame trader *needs* to execute his initiation order. For example, if you are on the 15-minute time frame from the buy side, and the hourly trader is nearing a buy signal, the hourly trader would like to see a sell signal on the 15-minute time frame in order to encourage a new 15-minute time frame short to open that he can buy from. Without knowing that the shorter time frame will be in conflict with the larger time frame at the exact moment the larger time frame is set to come in on the advancing side of the net order flow, you might be tempted to book a small gain in your time frame. Learn to let the larger time frames push your trade.

Know Your Profit Objective

If you don't know where you are going, you will probably end up someplace else.

—Yogi Berra

No trader will ever reach his full potential without some disciplined method of getting out of winners when it is time. The winning trade that continues to develop potential is a different issue. Profit objectives are necessary because you must have points in the market where you make choices. Sooner or later it is time to liquidate every trade and exit the market—the trade is over. When the time/price relationship reaches that point, you liquidate and wait for the next one.

The best time to make that choice is *before* you place your trade. Having a profit objective before you initiate provides good benefits for your developing trade methodology and your discipline. Profit objectives help you stay focused on getting paid the most from your winners.

Having a profit objective firmly in mind is crucial to lasting success for two basic reasons. First, it helps you maintain the proper risk-to-reward ratio on your open positions. As we discuss in detail later, the magic numbers are 42% winning trades and a 2:1 money won/lost ratio. At this level of performance you have a winning approach, but if you don't hold your winners you can't overcome your losers. Knowing how much money you are looking to take on any specific trade helps you keep your focus on this ratio. Just knowing these ratios and attempting to define your upside objective will keep you out of lower-probability trades. Placing your exit orders at or beyond price levels that will maintain this minimum winning ratio does not insure that those numbers will trade, of course, but having a resting order designed to take a profit allows you to benefit from winning ratios and helps you stay disciplined to take winners—to help your approach's inherent probabilities work for you more often than not.

Second, having a profit objective helps you fight the temptation to close a winner too early, cutting your profit short. As long as your trade is working, you have a better ability to sit tight; you are developing the much-needed discipline to leave a good thing alone. No matter how you want to slice it, no market will go straight up or straight down away from or toward your profit objective. It will take some amount of time for the trade to develop in order to eventually reach your objective. If you let every little switchback or price hiccup scare you out of your winners, you can't pay for your losers. Having an objective firmly in place will give you the perspective that is required to sit through and wait out temporary adverse price moves. Every market inhales and exhales.

Profit objectives are tools for effective trade management when holding your winners. They help you focus on finding good risk/reward ratios to begin with, but more important, they help you hold your winners for the largest potential gain. As long as you take the point of view that profit objectives are part of your tools, you will have more winners to start with that you can hold longer.

I have found a few helpful tools that allow me to remain confident in my profit objectives. First, look for a minimum three-to-one reward-to-risk ratio. This is not your actual price objective; this is the money you intend to risk compared to the market potential you hope to find. For example, if you believe that a market is developing a short-selling opportunity, where will you place your protective initial buy-stop order, and how far can the market go in your favor before the buyers step in and support it? If you are going to risk 50 points on a day trade, does the market have the potential to trade *at least* 150 lower on the day? If the answer is no, then you might want to pass on that particular short sale. You are looking for a high-quality relationship between your risk limit and your upside potential. If the market has never had a 150-point day in its entire history, then passing up that trade is a no-brainer; most likely the market doesn't have that much potential for the day. Your goal with a risk/reward ratio is to start from the premise that the ratio tells you how far the market must move if you take that position. Comparing your required profit objective to what you already know from your previous market study tells you better whether you really do have a potential trade with a higher or lower probability based on the parameters you have selected to trade with. You need to compare that risk with what you *have to get* if you take the position. In other words, if you can risk 50 points and the market can't pay you *at least* 150 (based on your study), knowing your required objective prevents you from placing a low-probability trade.

Having a profit objective also creates confidence to add to winning positions. Many trades will have much more profit potential than originally hoped for as they develop. When that potential becomes apparent, having an objective will help you ask good "if–then" questions to improve your net rate of return. When you see clearly that your original objective is only a small stopping point rather than the end of the trade, having a predetermined mind-set to add to the winning position is a great way to remain disciplined to work the winning trade until it is all over.

In my personal trading, I have two or three objectives for each position when I initiate for my first entry. The first objective is the area where I feel the market will have a pause, and a larger time frame trader must make a decision. For example, if I have bought an hourly low, my first objective would be the high of the day or previous day; that is most likely where the daily or weekly trader will take notice and either cap that rally with selling pressure or add to the net order flow on the buy side. No matter which happens, the first objective is not just price; it is time *and* price. I want to see the higher-time-frame trader push my trade with his order flow.

My second objective is the usual three-to-one reward/risk ratio. If I have correctly anticipated the net order flow, and the trader in the next higher time frame is joining the party, when the market gets to the *price* I am looking for I must decide if the trade has developed more potential in the same direction; that is a factor of *time*. If the rally has happened very quickly, and the market traded the second objective price and then backed off a bit, most likely that is stop-loss buying as the losing shorts cover and the larger time frame also liquidates. In this case, the rally may not have that much farther to go and I would either take the profit or at least roll a break-even protective stop. But if the rally took lots of time, there was good continued buying and selling from both sides as the objective was reached, and the price stayed at or around the objective for several hours, then it is possible that even larger time frames are coming into play. The entry of traders in the next larger time frame may mean that the potential for a further advance is still building. If the market continues to stay at or around the objective price while volume and open interest also increase, the market most likely has further to go. I would add to the position by some amount because the potential to reach the next objective has increased.

Should the market continue to advance after the position is added to, then the next objective level comes into play. That is usually a price area where the larger time frames take a stand from the other direction. For example, in this case, an hourly low was the right area to get long a market that has now made an advance that the daily or weekly trader is also interested in from the long side. As we approach the monthly opening range (for example), the monthly trader will now take notice. Since the market had been lower up until that point, the monthly trader is most likely either looking at placing shorts out, anticipating a failure of the month's opening range, or looking to go long if he is certain that the rally will continue. The net order flow will most likely start within a price/time relationship that includes everybody. Once the price reaches the monthly opening range, that price action will be a high on *everybody's* price chart.

So now we watch for the hourly price charts to show some selling, then the daily charts to show some selling, and finally the monthly charts. If the process takes 24 to 48 hours of clock time, and the market itself is lower for all those time frames, then most likely the traders in both the larger and the shorter time frames are all liquidating. The trade from the long side is running out of potential. The objective was reached and the trade is over.

However, if the price action continued to show strength—for example, the hourly price chart corrected lower and then prices returned to the high end of the range, the daily price chart closed near the high and just under the monthly opening range, it is a Friday afternoon and the profit-taking sell-off to close the week never happened, and so on—then the trade may be continuing to build potential. If the market advances further through the opening range, in this example, it would be a good time to add again to the position because traders in the larger time frame are now adding net order flow from the long side as well.

Having a series of profit objectives in place before you initiate the trade helps you to remain focused on the process of holding a winning trade. Markets are dynamic and conditions are always changing. Profit objectives help you maintain your edge for the simple reason that they keep your attention on the things that really matter: Changes in the net order flow as traders come in or leave the market. The important point of having a series of profit objectives is that you look for something changing at price/time points where it would make sense for something either to change or stay the same. As your objectives are reached, price action will provide important clues for you to review in order to have a degree of certainty about liquidating, holding, or adding to the winning position. But in all cases, price objectives are important areas to have predetermined in your mind. These are the places that you will do something or at least consider doing something. Whether the market ever trades to your price objectives or beyond them is really not important. It is important for a trader to remain proactive in his trade management.

Price objectives are stopping points that help you maintain focus on your trade. Having the price objective in mind before you place the trade will help you choose better-quality risk/reward ratios to start with. Having a series of objectives that are price- and time-sensitive and involve additional behavior from multiple time frames will help you get the most from your winners.

Don't Second-Guess Your Winners

In great affairs we ought to apply ourselves less to creating chances than to profiting from those that offer.

—François la Rochefoucauld,
Forbes Thoughts on Opportunity

Without a doubt, the most profitable market potential you can identify is a change in trend. When a market has stopped moving in one direction and is about to begin a move in the other direction, that potential might take time to fully develop but it is your lowest-risk, highest-probability opportunity. You are literally sitting on top of a gold mine. Getting in position early takes effort, but once you have established a base position, you need to let the trade work.

This is different from simply holding a winner. This is more an issue of maintaining proper focus, continuing to do the analysis needed to identify fundamental and technical potential, maintaining constant vigilance on net order flow as it changes, and sustaining a strong belief in yourself and your ability. Your trade hypothesis is developing and the time needed for a true change in trend to manifest might be quite long. The last thing you want to do is reevaluate what is happening and exit the trade early or, worse yet, reverse your position.

Personally, I can show you trade records where I have been at the précis point in both time and price to be long or short from the change in trend, sometimes from a yearly or multiyear high or low. Did I get paid? Yes, but not what I could have. I second-guessed my hypothesis.

Looking back, I can see that it was mostly because I lacked the focus and discipline to just leave well enough alone. What stands out in my mind most is the high in the orange juice market for 1991. I was short from $2.06/Lb. I covered at around $1.95/Lb. Yes, I made a nice gain on the trade, but within a year that market was over 50 cents a pound lower.

During the time the market was under selling pressure, I kept looking for another short position to put out on a rally. I convinced myself that the initial break was too fast and that a re-test of the highs was coming. But that rally never happened. Because I was content to book a nice gain instead of just letting the trade work, I missed one of the truly great short positions of the last decade or so. My trade hypothesis was the correct one and my initial timing was good, but I second-guessed myself. True, a lot of that was inexperience, but that is the whole purpose of developing trading rules that work: to place controls on your behavior until you can trade with enough discipline to *let profits run*.

Rule #14, "Don't second guess your winners," is first cousin to Rule #11 and a critical part of letting profits run. Of the mistakes many traders make, the mistake of second-guessing themselves is the most costly. Not only will they be out of the market when prices continue to advance favorably for their initial trade hypothesis, but often these same traders make the most costly mistake of all by second guessing themselves: Trying to be on both sides of the market. If you want to watch your trading stake go up in smoke as fast as possible, I recommend you try to trade both sides of a market that is developing a trend.

Because the temptation of unlimited profit potential is so strong, many traders attempt to trade from both the long side and the short side of a market that has true potential in only one of those directions. This is a common mistake to make after a market has made a hefty advance in one direction, because we all know a correction is coming and it will be a big one. For example, if you are long soybeans from the seasonal bottom at the end of the year and on into the spring, and if the market has advanced 80¢/BU up to planting, it is reasonable to expect a top may be in place if the acreage planted is higher than expected. It would not be uncommon for sellers to come in and for holders of open longs to liquidate at least some of their positions. Under those trading conditions, a 30 to 40¢/BU drop in price would not be uncommon, and that drop might take a week or longer to play out. If you are holding a nice open-trade gain on open longs, you might be tempted to liquidate and reverse with the intention of reestablishing longs after the correction, taking a gain from the short side as well.

The problem is, in this case, you might be shorting a bull market. Remember, it is the blood of the shorts that have been paying the bulls. You have now placed yourself on the side of the market that has *already proven to be the losing side*. Yes, a 40¢/BU correction is a lot of money, and yes, that correction would work against an open-trade profit. But the risk you are taking by second-guessing your original bullish hypothesis is that you will not time your participation well. In most cases, the anticipated correction will not happen exactly as expected, nor will it be precisely a certain amount, *if* underlying bullish conditions remain. If conditions remain bullish for a change in trend, and that uptrend has another three months to go, you won't know that for certain until later, but your new short position is in serious jeopardy. If those bullish conditions remain after a bearish fundamental is ignored or absorbed, it will only take one rally to take away a good portion of your previously closed gain *and* you won't have a position of any kind once you liquidate your losing shorts. A $1.50/BU price change in favor of the bullish hypothesis going forward might mean little or no gain to your account if you don't have your original base longs still working—you were short for a time against the trend and you were flat for a time, waiting to reestablish your longs that would have worked anyway.

All of this could have been avoided by holding to your original hypothesis and letting your positions work until that market was clearly over from the long side. By second-guessing yourself, you took money out of you own pocket when *your hypothesis was the correct one*.

Now, I'm not suggesting that you will see a $1.50/BU up-move in soybeans every year. Obviously, seasonal tendencies in the grain complex are different from year to year; I am not postulating that bullish or bearish trades will play out as anticipated under all market conditions. I am simply using an illustration. My intention is to show you that *no matter how* you come to a conclusion that a market has potential in one direction over another, you serve your self-interest best by staying with that hypothesis and not vacillating. You need to consider trading only from that side in most cases, and you need to find a way to leave your initial position on long enough for the potential you have found to develop fully. That could take time.

The psychology behind this rule is critical for your lasting success, because following this rule helps you follow all the other rules for letting profits run. If you second-guess yourself and your trade hypothesis, most likely you will cut an open-trade profit short, you will not add to your winners, and you will not have a profit objective you are willing to wait for. When you second-guess yourself you lose the benefit of using multiple time frames and of course, your records show that your personal results data remains inconclusive for true learning of your strengths and weaknesses. At best, changing quickly from one hypothesis to another prevents you from finding the truly profitable trades that make all the difference; and at worst, it prevents you from getting paid the highest return for the risk you are assuming. One reason short-time-frame traders never achieve the lasting success that long-term traders more often have is because the short-time-frame trader is not holding to a perspective that pays the most: identifying a change in trend and sticking with it.

To make this rule work, you as a trader need to be prepared to make additional choices for the long-term health of your trading account. To earn the highest rate of return possible, you need to prepare ahead of time certain trading behaviors and be ready to apply them. When a trade hypothesis is working and your initial base position is showing a profit, be prepared to ask the question, "How far could this go?" If you are willing to consider that your initial price objective may be only a small part of what might prove to be a huge move, you must be willing to consider entering from the same side again very quickly if you liquidate. Perhaps adding to the position as the market passes your objective is a better move. If you are remaining vigilant in your personal market study and your record keeping, perhaps you see that something is changing and your original trade hypothesis is more accurate than ever; in this case, holding at least some of your position is a better play.

This rule works for your best potential when you have the capacity to hold to your first conclusion and are willing to stay with it for as long as it takes. When you look at some past market moves, trends that lasted for years in some cases, there are always traders who were there and on the right side at the turns—when the risk was lowest and the profit potential greatest. Some were even there by accident. But as the trades developed, those very same traders chose to change their hypothesis for reasons of their own, either liquidating long before the full potential was realized or even entering positions from the other side and suffering losses. By remaining in the frame of mind not only that you can be positioned at the turns but also that you can hold those positions, add to them, and wait for the trend to fully develop without taking yourself out of the game early, you will be in position to hit the home run. But if you let the short-term fluctuations or pullbacks convince you that the trade is no longer going to work, or convince you that the trend has failed, you are not trading the net order flow or the market potential—you are merely trading your personal point of view. Your goal in making this rule work for you is to learn what you need to learn about your market first and be willing to give the market as much time as it needs for that trade to develop.

By combining the essential elements of "letting profits run" into an effective trade management technique, you will gain the confidence you need to sit tight on a winning trade and let traders in the other time frames come to the same conclusion and add order flow in that direction; and you will create the discipline required to hold for the objective. All the time this is happening, you are watching for more clues that this is really the beginning of a bigger development in the same direction. When you see that potential fully, you can then add to the winner and easily wait for the next objective.

Over time, as you practice holding winners and letting profits run, you will learn that the markets are a very big place. There are times when the hugeness of the move won't be seen at all by anyone at the start and only a handful of traders will have positions on. Once that trend develops and becomes clear to everyone, that power from the net order flow will push that trade farther than you might have initially expected. Remaining open to that possibility *right from the start* increases your probability for a windfall gain. If a change in trend is truly developing, those clues will show, and you need to be open to the possibility that you were in the right place at the right time; now you need to run with it.

Traders who have the ability to let a profit run are always the traders with an open mind to the possibility that anything can develop. Once they are on the right side they are looking for clues that this position might go a very long way. They tend to stay with that potential until the market has said either yes or no, but they rarely second-guess their initial hypothesis for the simple reason that it apparently was the correct one. Rather, they ask the question, "How right *could* this be?" If their initial trade hypothesis is the correct one, and it turns out to be the correct one for years, they will most likely have some trades on all the time. But they made that choice before the trade was entered. Those traders took the point of view that anything can develop, and if it does, and they are on the right side, they are sticking with it.

PART IV

Trader Maxims

Know the Limits of Your Analysis

Every ship at the bottom of the ocean has a set of charts on it.

—Old nautical saying

When I first started trading in May 1986, the first book I read on the markets was *Chart Your Way to Stock Market Profits*, by David L. Markstein (New York: Arco Publishing, 1972). I have since lost the book and I couldn't find it again searching the Web. I probably threw it out, now that I have a better grasp on what I am doing every day. About the only thing I remember about the book was how intoxicating it felt to read something for the first time that provided me with such a simple solution to my goal of getting rich in the markets. I was too uneducated (some would say naive) to understand that it wasn't going to be that simple. There were numerous books and services available for people interested in trading equities, but there was very little data available specifically for traders interested in futures or options. The cash FOREX markets were the exclusive domain of banks and private investors, so that market wasn't even available. For me as a new trader, the best course of action was to actually go to work in the industry and learn the business from the inside out. So I did.

After I began trading—and accumulating losses—I continued to ravenously devour anything I could find on market analysis. At the time, the alleged science of technical analysis was still in its infancy. Most of the technical indicators that are used by traders today were just concepts. Commonly used indicators such as Williams %R, MACD, and the commodity channel index (CCI) had not been developed or were not licensed to all the available charting services. Many indicators were formulas you had to compute manually and then physically mark the results on a paper chart. At the time, having a real-time data feed from the exchanges was very costly and required dedicated computer hardware. There was no online access to information like there is today, and you needed an actual broker available to place trades and report fills. All of what we take for granted today as a professional-level, online market presence literally had not been invented yet; and this was only 20 years ago. (As a side note, I actually met George Lane, the developer of stochastics, at the Chicago Board of Trade just after I began working full-time in the markets in 1987. He was considered a god at the time.)

I continued to read, study, chart, and trade for years, spending huge sums of money on real-time data feeds, books, audio courses, charting services, live seminars, and so on. During this educational experience, *at no time* did any of these self-created gurus ever mention that the futures and options markets were zero-sum transactions. The only exposure I initially had to the concept of zero-sum transactions was when I passed my Series III brokers exam. I didn't know how critical that information would be until after I had my first blowout. In fact, when I teach my "Psychology of Trading" seminar today, there is always at least one person in the audience who has been trading for years but has never even heard the term and has no clue what it means. The inherent nature of zero-sum transactions makes analysis of the markets a very different thing than the analysts and chartists would have you believe.

During this part of my development as a trader I continued to have net losses. I searched and searched for the cause of my losses, believing, like most novices do, that the problem must be at least in part due to how I was doing my analysis. What made this period so frustrating for me was that the root problem was exactly that—how I was doing my market analysis—but *real* analysis of the markets has very little to do with technical analysis or technical indicators. Knowing that difference is what made all the education come together for me. You need to know that difference as well, or your results will remain net losses, because zero-sum transactions cannot be mathematically analyzed nor predicted with any certainty. Proponents of technical analysis methods will have a field day with that statement, but I am going to show you something that will help you understand that the limits of technical analysis, when properly viewed in the context of zero-sum transactions, are the very thing that makes it valuable.

The very nature of zero-sum transactions means that exactly 50% of executed contracts have profit potential. Once the net order flow has moved the traded price away from the executed entry, it is impossible for both of the open positions to show a profit. Without advance knowledge of the net order flow, your actual mathematical probability for a winning trade once you have executed for your entry is 50%. Bear in mind, I am not using any trading hypothesis, analysis, or previous support/resistance information. I am merely stating the fact that once the market moves, you will have either an open-trade profit or a loss at that point. We are not discussing the market "coming back," the potential to make a new yearly high/low, chart formations that have probabilities, or anything else. I am saying that from a mathematical point of view, it is impossible for everybody to be right.

The idea behind technical analysis is that by somehow combining or dividing previously traded prices, overlaying a type of constant algorithm to previously traded prices, comparing previously traded prices to some formula, and so on, you can thereby arrive at a number that the market has a potential to reach, predict the market will change direction, or be confident that it will continue in the same direction. The seduction of your will is now complete and you place yourself at risk.

But the market continues to move for the only reason that it will ever move—because of the net order flow. Most traders now believe that if you have an open-trade loss after this mental dance of technical analysis has been done, somehow the analysis was not done correctly—otherwise, they would have been on the other side or waited. This illusion is what most traders operate under for the entire life of their trading career. The more firmly entrenched a trader is in this illusion, the greater amount of study or analysis he will do or the greater amount of money he will spend trying to develop a better technical approach.

The important bedrock understanding you as a trader need to have about technical analysis is that it is not *predictive*; it is *historical*. Technical analysis *cannot* predict price action because it is mathematically impossible for everybody to be right in the first place, and everyone has the same technical analysis available to them.

A price chart with a 21-bar moving average and stochastics on my desk is *identical* to your price chart with a 21-bar moving average and stochastics on your desk. If we both conclude the same thing—that this data predicts a price rise, for example—and every other trader in the world using that same technical analysis sees the same thing we have been taught to glean from it, and we all decide to buy *because we trust the analysis*, the only way we can get into that market is if someone sells to us. What is the seller using to conclude that the time to get in is also now but that the market is poised to move lower? What is his analysis based on?

The really seductive part of this whole process is that if the trade makes a profit, the trader *assumes the analysis works*. That is the conclusion most traders will come to. The only reason the trade worked is because the net order flow was from that side, but the trader concludes it was the analysis that found the trade. Once the analysis works *one time*, the trader extrapolates that to mean it will work *all the time*. If using the exact same analysis again results in a loss, the trader assumes the fault was in how the analysis was done. In other words, the crystal ball wasn't plugged in this time. But the trader is still convinced that he owns a crystal ball.

If you do your homework you will discover that any form of technical analysis has some level of probability of finding a winning trade. For the most part, all technical analysis or mathematical models developed for systemized use have a success rate between 38% and 52% winning trades based on the predictive hypothesis used by the developer. That is no better than chance. If you flip a coin 100 times you will have 52% heads or tails, or some random bell curve distribution based on probability theory. In fact, the entire industry based on this predictive illusion of technical analysis is very proud to document to you the winning trade to losing trade ratio of the system in question. If you want a real eye-opener, just count how many of these high-tech, systemized approaches have win/loss ratios lower than the 35% range, which is actually less than flipping a coin. What are these people thinking?

Since technical analysis will only help you 52% of the time *at best*, why would you trust it 100% of the time?

Answering that question and really *thinking* about what you are doing is the key to following this rule. You must know the limits of your analysis and what the analysis is really saying in order to use it successfully. In my opinion, the simplest way to effectively use technical analysis is to look at it from the loser's point of view.

Proper analysis of your market starts with the understanding that not all of the participants are going to be winners. The loser is in there somewhere and he must liquidate at some point. Looking at the market price action from the point of view that the loser is in there, thinking and trusting *something* that allows him to place himself at risk, puts you in a position to *anticipate* potential net order flow when it is about time for the loser to quit. Your best analysis is done by asking the question, "Where is the loser?"

The last thing you want your analysis to do is attempt to predict price action. You want your analysis to disclose *historical* information. You want information that discloses where the loser is, what he is most likely thinking, and where he will most likely be forced to liquidate the losing trade. You already know that the loser has trusted some form of analysis, he is using it to *predict* price action, and he can't be right. Armed with that point of view, you need to assess at what point a loser would come into the market and where he would most likely liquidate. All of your technical analysis is best used to help uncover where the loser is and what he is most likely thinking in order to continually keep placing himself at risk. Your analysis is best used to help you understand *what has already happened* and then help you deduce *what must happen next*.

This is a different process than predicting price action. The process of critical deduction, intuition, and knowledge combined with the question "Where is the loser?" is not predictive. You really don't need to answer the question, "Which price is coming next?" You need to answer the question "Where and when will the loser quit?"

Before we conclude this discussion on the limits and usefulness of technical analysis, I think it is best to make a few things clear so no one gets the wrong impression. I am not saying that technical analysis is bad or that it is without value. There are many parts of technical analysis that are very useful and should be part of a well-rounded trading methodology. I think you would be best served in your use of technical analysis if you would not trust it implicitly to find winning trades. I believe that it is best used in conjunction with sound knowledge of what ultimately drives prices.

Net order flow can only change if someone is certain enough that he will make a winning trade and he is willing to initiate a position to find out. Regardless of all the little nuances that happen around the net order flow or the degree of probability one kind of analysis has versus another, the bottom line is that only a fraction of open contracts will be on the right side of the price action long enough to have a profit. Technical analysis is designed to uncover this inequality, but charts cannot tell you what will happen. Charts and analysis can only provide a detailed history of what has already happened. It is up to the trader doing the analysis to deduce what is most likely to happen next from that historical information.

Trade with the Trend

The trend is your friend.
—Edwin Lefèvre, *Reminiscences of a Stock Operator*

Anyone who has traded for more than one day in his life knows this rule. As a factor in managing risk/reward ratio and playing it smart, most traders attempt to trade with the trend currently in progress. Identifying a trend in progress is rather easy. If we set aside all the other parts of a trading approach, things like how to get positioned properly, limiting losses, adding to a winner, and so on, and focus on just this one rule for a moment, we have only one thing we need to be concerned with: the direction, or trend, of the market.

WHAT IS A TREND?

A trend is usually defined in the markets as a general direction that net prices are moving. There are three kinds of trends, and all of them can be highly profitable when traded properly. All three kinds of trends have a beginning and an end. Additionally, the end of one trend usually signals the start of the next trend. I personally believe that identifying the end of a trend is the single most profitable trading tool you can develop. The end of the current trend is the best place to liquidate an open-trade winner and/or initiate a new position at the beginning of the new trend, when the risk is lowest and the profit potential is greatest.

The three types of trends are *uptrend, downtrend,* and *range.* Obviously, an uptrend, as shown in Figure 16.1, is a series of prices where the high prices keep getting higher and the low prices are marked higher, too. Figure 16.2 clearly shows a downtrend, while a range is illustrated in Figure 16.3.

Making this rule work for you requires a willingness to identify *what is already happening* and simply assume that it will continue for at least the time you are in at least one trade. You also need to decide whether your trading methodology will work for each kind of trend. Some systemized approaches or technical methods are *trend followers* and some are *breakout* or *momentum identifiers.* Breakout or momentum approaches are not good for initiating positions with an existing up or downtrend; they are not designed to remain in a market long enough for the trend to resume and create a profit. Breakout or momentum approaches are best used when a market has been in a range for a period of time. When the range is over, that is usually signaled by a large move in one direction or the other.

If you intend to trade with the prevailing trend as part of your trade

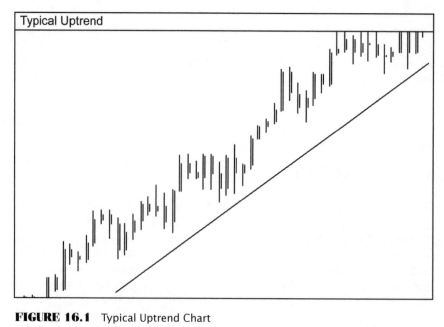

FIGURE 16.1   Typical Uptrend Chart

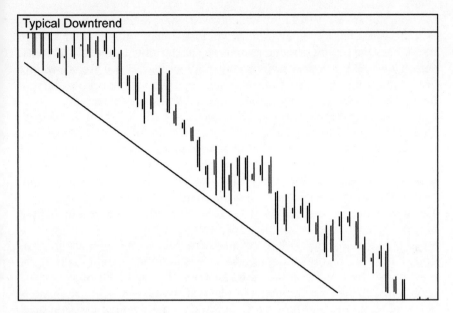

FIGURE 16.2 Typical Downtrend Chart

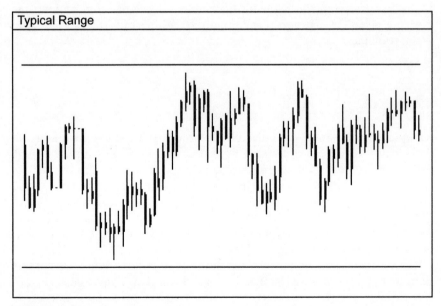

FIGURE 16.3 Typical Range Chart

method, make sure you know which trend your method is designed for. Systems designed for range trading will lose money on any other kind of trend, because trading a range assumes a shorter time frame and often assumes you will use a *close and reverse* methodology. If you are not willing to be long from the bottom of the range and then short back down from the top, then a range trading system may not work as well for you.

No matter which trend you choose to trade, the common-sense psychology behind this rule is "Don't argue with the market." Figures 16.1 through 16.3 all clearly indicate which prevailing trend is evident, and you should be able to determine the right side for initiating a position without a lot of argument. As a trader looking for long-term success, one of the important disciplines to learn is that the market is always right. The market very clearly says what the prevailing trend is, and taking money from a market no matter which trend is evident does not require a lot of effort, study, or work. It requires discipline. Once you are in position along with the prevailing trend, there is nothing to do but add to the position as the trend continues. Regardless of your initial objective for liquidation, if the trend remains in place and a further price advance is developing, there is nothing to do but add to the winning position until the trend is over.

Before we discuss clues to discovering the end of a trend, I would like to discuss each trend individually. Each kind of trend has some unique underlying behavior that needs to be understood in order to take less risk when trading it.

UPTREND

An uptrend is the most difficult to trade successfully. Finding a market at a critical or significant low price does not insure that a bull market will ever develop. But if it does, bull markets are actually aberrations and exploited by professional traders as a short-term situation that provides a short-selling opportunity. The more convinced the typical trader is that a bull market is under way, the better the short-selling potential for the professional. It is no accident that most fortunes in futures and options have been made by short-selling.

When discussing bull markets in futures and options, it is important to note that equities are not included in this discussion. Equities are *investments*, not *speculation*. The underlying reasons for a bull market in stocks are almost never the reasons for a bull market in other markets. Equities are not zero-sum markets, so the forces that create price action are different. Unlike the 50/50 relationship between long and short positions in zero-sum markets, short interest in equities typically is never more than 5 to 8%, even in raging bear markets.

There are no bull and bear markets in FOREX, either. True, you may be long or short one currency from the point of view of the other, but that is a function of *relative value*, not bullish or bearish. Currencies are not money in the truest sense of the word. The currency markets have always been subject to some stable store of value throughout history (such as gold), and only in the last 50 years or so has the stable store of value relationship changed. All currencies devalue over time, regardless of whether they rise or fall faster against one another for a period of time. A bull market in currencies is not possible, even though one currency may gain value briefly against another.

If you intend to be long a market for a developing uptrend, you must be prepared to consider that a shorter-term trade. Bull markets attract a lot of noise and people who normally would never be in that market. For example, in 1988 I traded the grain complex during the Midwest drought. At the height of the price advance, over half my customers buying grains had never traded in any market before. Many had bought only because they saw it on the news every day and simply couldn't pass up a supposedly sure thing. The entire bull market was over in four months, and the grains haven't traded those prices again since. Bull markets are exhaustive in nature and are often subject to manias, panics, and nonprofessional participation, much more so than other trends.

As a developing trader, part of your best approach for trading an uptrend is the point of view that "All of this could be over tomorrow. There is no such thing as a bull market." Always be hyper-vigilant on a long position when trading an uptrend. Bull markets make me nervous.

DOWNTREND

Trading in a downtrend is the most secure and profitable way to increase your account balance. Once the pressure comes on, that market could go a long way and be under downtrend for years and years. Contrary to uptrends, bear markets need very little to keep them going; hence the old trader's phrase, "A bull has to eat every day but a bear only needs to eat once in a while" (referring to news and additional new traders coming in). I say more about bear markets in Rule #24.

A downtrend always follows an uptrend. It is the nature of zero-sum transaction markets that any bull market will be followed by an equal or greater bear market. If your trading approach is to include short-selling, then any bull market needs to be closely monitored for the inevitable change in trend that will occur. It is only a matter of time, and if you are prepared properly you will make an absolute fortune on the short side if you are willing to remain disciplined and add to that short over time. As I mentioned earlier, the grains have never traded back to the highs seen during the bull market in the spring of 1988. A properly positioned short would still be making money years after the highs in June of that year. If you want to really get serious about trading and you want to make this rule work for you, look for an equal or greater number of downtrends in your regular analysis and trade selection.

RANGE

Trading in a range is the easiest money available to you. There is a lower risk of being early on the buy or sell side, which could occur when the market is in an uptrend or downtrend. No matter how you slice it, you could buy a low market a little too early or sell a high market a little too soon. In a range trade, the buying and selling points are already predetermined for you. Your only real question is whether the range is over the moment you execute one way or the other for the first time.

I have found that range is the most profitable trading opportunity for short-term trading. A market typically will trade in an established range through at least three or four attempts to seek a new higher or lower equilibrium. In other words, once the range is established, there is a very low risk of a breakout in either direction for usually two solid attempts from the buy side or the sell side of the range. You simply buy the lower 5% of the established range and sell the upper 5% of the established range. If you are aggressive you can close your longs and reverse, attempting to capture both sides.

Range trades are more common in shorter time frames such as the 120-minute or less. Almost all uptrends or downtrends experience periods of range lasting from several hours to several weeks while continuing the overall advance or decline. Some traders establish base positions on the uptrend or downtrend and then, when range is apparent, trade short-term from the same side until the overall trend resumes. Then they add to the open trend-following position.

BENEFITS OF CLEARLY APPRAISING TREND

Uptrends, downtrends, and ranges occur with regular frequency, and each offers better money-making potential when it ends. Once an uptrend ends, it will be followed by a downtrend very quickly. A range at the end of an uptrend is less common than before the end of a downtrend. A range will end in a continuation of an uptrend or downtrend more often than not. In other words, the prevailing bull or bear market usually continues a bit further once a range has been evident for a short time. When a downtrend ends, it is usually followed by a range for some time. Very rarely does a downtrend end and an uptrend immediately begin, forming a "V" bottom at a significant low price. In most middle-priced markets, the process of trend identification goes like this: range, resumption of uptrend/downtrend, range.

The end of an uptrend or downtrend is the most profitable time because the risk is low and profit potential high just before prices reverse into the change in trend. Identifying a change in trend from up to down (or vice versa) is easy in hindsight because the price chart will clearly show you the directional change. But in most cases, if the event is about to happen in a middle-priced market—a market that is not at a significant high or low, (such as a 10-year price level)—then there will be some period of range just before the turn. If volume and open interest have declined during this period of range at the end of an uptrend or downtrend, there is a high probability a reversal is in the works. See Figure 16.4.

FIGURE 16.4 Change in Trend: Uptrend Followed by Range prior to Downtrend. USD/CHF Cash Spot FOREX, April 17, 2005, to April 17, 2006. Courtesy of G.T.S. Charting.

The important thing to remember about this rule is that each of the three potential trends available has unique characteristics. Developing a solid trading method is all about fitting your personal trading approach into the most comfortable kind of trend for you. I personally have worked with traders who, after learning enough about the market psychology and their personal psychology, have decided to only trade one kind of trend rather than try to trade all potential price action. As a matter of fact, the highest performers have always been short-sellers working in downtrends or the sell-side of ranges.

Use Effective Money Management

Success does not depend upon having enough capital but in deploying it properly.
—Frank A. Taucher

Every trader at one time or another has made the mistake of improper equity allocation. By that I mean trading too large or too small, adding to a losing trade, cutting a profit short, or failing to add to a winning trade. In reality, equity allocation is not a function of trade management. It is a function of understanding who is taking risk and who is using the market for what purpose. Very few traders have fully understood the relationship between *real risk* and *perceived risk*. Even fewer know that properly *assuming risk* to begin with is the key to building a healthy balance.

Many books have been written on proper money management. Most of them start with the premise that taking an unreasonable risk is where all the woe in your portfolio comes from. Many successful investors have well-diversified portfolios and have various percentages in low-risk, medium-risk, and high-risk investments. The underlying assumption is that the more risk you take, the worse your potential gains will be. If you look deeper at the issue of money management, you discover that the real problem is who is managing the wealth and what they are thinking.

I know many people who have what they consider to be well-diversified portfolios. They have 40% or so of their money in low-yield places like municipal bonds or U.S. debt. They have 30% or so of their money in places like growth stocks or investment real estate. The rest is spread out between things like start-up business ventures or cutting-edge opportunities like bio-tech or alternative energy stocks. Basically, as far as I can tell, they are content to preserve their capital and hope for the best. They don't want a lot of risk.

All of these various "secure" or "less risky" investments boil down to *someone else in control.* If I buy a stock investment, for example, the potential growth to my capital investment is actually going to be determined by how effective the management team of that particular company is. If it turns out that the management team is unresponsive to the underlying business climate, the potential for that company to continue growing market share (and stock value) diminishes. If I invest in some kind of bond, the interest rate depends on how long I leave that capital in someone else's hands. If a city government wants to build a new highway and raises the cash from a bond sale, that city will make more money over time than it will pay me in interest, and it may require me to keep the bond for decades.

All of this is well understood by professional money managers, and those individuals have mountains of data designed to maximize yield and minimize risk. They have huge amounts of capital allocated across as many different market opportunities as possible and they pay the yield to *you,* the investor (less any fees). As the investor, you must be content to receive whatever gain that particular money manager's skill set is capable of earning. The professional money manager is not a risk taker. He is a risk avoider.

For us as traders the game is completely different. We are looking to exploit some perceived opportunity when we see the current market price as too high or too low relative to some other price we are expecting to see trade down the road. We start from the premise that the risk is certainly worth taking. But knowing the perfect price/time relationship to assume that risk is the difficult part. In my view, we have this problem because we don't know that asset allocation and money management are for *investments,* not trading. Trading is about getting paid for a risk someone else doesn't want to take.

If you study wealthy individuals who started with nothing, you will discover there is a common thread behind all of them. They all take control of their finances and allocate resources differently than the average person. They assume risk others will not—and the lion's share of profits goes to them. Most of the self-made wealthy people have discovered that *people will pay to avoid risk.* This is also where the concept of *other people's money* comes into play. Without question, the proper use of your capital will lead to using someone else's capital, thereby creating leverage for the risk taker. In the markets we call that *margin.* If you are trading crude oil, for example, the total contract value is much larger than the cash deposit needed to control that contract. That crude oil is somewhere in the world for the time you control it. Someone is willing to let the price change either for or against him, and one of those someones is a hedger. Knowing when hedgers are active in the market leads to knowing how to properly allocate capital.

A hedger's goal is to transfer risk to the speculator. *You* are the speculator. When the hedger feels it is time to transfer risk to you, it is time to allocate your capital and take the risk. Properly use of your capital begins with *accepting risk*. Individual traders who hope to profit without assuming a lot of risk are setting themselves up for a trading disaster. Trading the markets cannot be done successfully unless you assume risk. When someone who does not want the risk is active, you have a time/price relationship that has a very good chance of being a place to assume risk. The key is understanding that low rates of return are paid to non–risk takers, and high rates of return are paid to risk takers.

Using our crude oil example, when a hedger *sells* into the market, that particular hedger *sells* crude oil because he believes a price decline is possible, even likely. By using the markets to hedge he is saying, "I don't want to risk a price decline." Who would be most likely to know if a price decline was possible? Wouldn't that be someone in the business of *selling* crude oil for a living? The moment the hedger becomes active, you have a very good clue that it is time to allocate capital and assume the risk that the hedger does not want. You now take your capital and *leverage his knowledge*.

Now, I am not saying that you should sell into the crude oil market just because the hedgers are selling crude oil today. I am saying that properly allocating your capital begins by knowing who does not want the risk in the market, and accepting that risk. In most cases, simply knowing the price levels at which the hedgers say, "That's enough" gives you the best place to begin using your capital. Effective money management begins with assuming the right risk at the right time. The rest is academic.

Why is this point of view the cornerstone to effective money management? Because the markets are designed for the hedger and not the speculator. The speculator is attempting to profit from a perception of price *potential*. The hedger is using *actual* prices. In most cases the hedger is looking for a change in price when he participates. If the price change does not occur he is not harmed. If the price change does occur, he is protected and he provided you the opportunity to benefit from that change. In most cases, hedging activity will stop a price advance or decline, or at least delay it. Knowing when and where hedgers are active provides important clues for when it is time for you to take the *actual risk* and the benefit your account.

The *perception* of risk is what most money management concerns itself with and this perception of risk is what most traders focus on. They want to play but they don't want to pay. There is only one risk in the market: that you may be on the wrong side of the net order flow. You can perceive that situation immediately by the very next traded price, so perception of risk is not really a concern—except for the trader who is ignorant of or unwilling to accept the actual net order flow. What you want to avoid is executing for your initial position in a place that is of no interest to the person who ultimately receives the best benefit from the markets. You do not want to buy and sell from other speculators. You want to either buy or sell with the hedger or against the hedger; but you want to avoid participating against other speculators for the most part.

Once you are accepting the risk others do not want, and the market is moving favorably for your initial position, the rest of proper money management comes into play, but this is only valuable because you still have your original money to begin with. If you have been trading for a reasonable amount of time and a reasonable number of trades but your equity is lower than your starting balance, the only thing you need to discover is how to get on the right side of the net order flow more often. One valuable clue is knowing when hedgers are active, because they will execute to avoid risk only at price areas that are *actually important.* The fact that most speculators are losers means that a certain amount of them will be available for the hedger to square off with. Who is more likely to win, John Q. Public or Cargill, when both are trading in the wheat market?

Once you have a winning position working, you must allocate more resources to the winner. The four basic rules for money management at that point are as follows:

1. Roll protective stops to the break-even point.
2. Purchase options to lock profits.
3. Add to the winner on pullbacks.
4. Scale out when hedgers from the other side become active.

I have found that a 1.5% equity risk on initiation of the position will keep you in the game until you have found the winner and have a lead on the trade. Using options to lock profits will free up equity to add to the winner. When hedgers from the other side are active, the limits to the playing field are established and liquidating some or all of the position is advisable.

Now, I know most traders were expecting this rule to be a discussion of ratios, percents, stop placement, and so on. In the Introduction I pointed out that making the rules work depends on understanding the psychology behind the rules and adapting that psychology to your personal trading approach. The psychology behind using effective money management is first and foremost preserving your capital until you find the winning trade. That's easy enough; don't risk more than about 1.5% of your starting balance on any one trade. Once you have a lead on the winner, you add to it and *let it work*. You liquidate when the net order flow dries up in that direction. You are looking to initiate when the net order flow is set to change, and you are looking to liquidate when it changes again. In between those two points you are looking to add to your winner and lower your open-trade risk, either by rolling stops or buying options against your futures.

The best way to effectively manage your equity is to look for the risk no one else wants to begin with. That is usually a price level that is of interest to hedgers. The rest is common sense.

Know Your Ratios

How did I get rich? Well, I sold apples to start. I bought a dozen apples wholesale for 50¢, polished them real nice and sold them for 10¢ a piece. I kept at it until I had well over $3,000 in profits. Then my uncle died and left me $1.4 million.
—Henny Youngman, comedian

Every business has ratios. Every business has expenses and incomes. Every business has market share, and every business has profit and loss opportunities. Trading is a business just like any other, and part of your long-term success as a trader will come from knowing exactly what your business balance sheet looks like. You must know your expenses and incomes, you must know your market share, and you must know your profit or loss relationships. You must know your ratios.

Ratios provide important clues to the *actual performance* of your trading. When I teach my "Psychology of Trading" seminar, it still amazes me that some traders have no details or printed records of their recent trade results to show me. They cannot tell me what their performance is. These traders have only one piece of information available: the balance in their trading account. That would be like running a corner bakery with only one piece of information each day: your checking account balance. No knowledge of your expenses, your utilities, cost of raw materials, profit margin on a loaf of bread—nothing. Imagine running a business that way. Most traders are running their trading business in exactly that manner. They have few or no records with which to get the true picture of how well their business is performing.

Accurate record keeping and regular calculation of your ratios will provide you with important information that will give you several solid benefits. First, by knowing your actual performance from day to day you will see more clearly how well you are following the rules you have created for yourself. Next, knowing your performance ratios gives you clues as to what areas of your daily trade presence need to improve. Last, and probably the most important information, you will have more data available when you are about to make a serious mistake. Knowing the performance you are creating in real time creates a sound understanding of what you need to do from that point forward. No trader gets to be at the top of his game without regular and critical review of his moment-to-moment performance.

Every trader has distinct parts of his trade approach that require more focus than others. In my case, I am subject to a tendency to overtrade. I need to critically review my daily execution regularly because if I am not careful I will easily break discipline in this area. I have no problem holding a winner. So for me, a regular assessment of my execution records is very helpful because overtrading usually results in losses. My records have provided clues when I am about to start overtrading, and more often than not I can head that off at the pass. In a worst-case scenario, I have a rule that I have learned is a critical part of my discipline, and I follow it every day. I developed that rule because I discovered my tendency to overtrade by critically examining my trade records regularly.

Once you have disciplined yourself to keep accurate records, you need to begin calculating your ratios. Regardless of how you want to slice it, because we operate in an arena that is subject to a degree of uncertainty, a portion of our net results is a function of probabilities. We cannot know in advance with absolute certainty that we will be on the right side of the net order flow. Once we execute, we are going to have a gain or a loss. A portion of those results will be due to chance, either for or against our account balance. If we are maintaining a strong market focus and a solid level of discipline we can tip that percentage in our favor. The magic numbers are 42% winning trades to losing trades combined, with a 2:1 profit-to-loss ratio. These numbers are a factor of the *probability of ruin matrix*, illustrated in Figure 18.1.

The probability of ruin matrix is a calculation based on several pieces of data. First, it assumes 100 events; in this case that would be 100 trades. Next, it defines ruin as a 50% drawdown from starting equity. Last, it assumes that the methodology used to initiate each event is always the same

		\multicolumn{7}{c}{Percent}						
		30	35	40	45	50	55	60
	1:1	99	88	88	73	50	27	12
	1.5:1	98	85	50	17	4	1	0
Profit/Loss Ratio	2:1	74	38	14	5	2	1	0
	2.5:1	40	17	7	3	1	1	0
	3:1	23	11	5	3	1	1	0
	3.5:1	17	8	5	3	1	1	0
	4:1	14	8	5	3	1	1	0

FIGURE 18.1 Probability of Ruin Matrix
Ruin is defined as a 50 percent drawdown from starting equity.

in every event; in other words, each trade done during the 100 trades in the sample set is executed for exactly the same reason.

According to this matrix, if you do 100 trades, and have 42% winners, and pull two dollars out for every dollar you give back, your probability of ruin is a little less than 14%. If you calculate the numbers yourself you will find that $(42 \times 2) - (58 \times 1)$ actually yields a profit of $26, but the ruin matrix is using the full scope of probability theory. That includes the possibility that all the losing trades will come in the first 58 executions, or enough of them that your equity draws down 50% before the sample set of 100 trades is complete.

Notice that a high percentage of winning trades is not an indication that you will make money net in your account. Someone who has 55% winning trades to losing trades has a worse risk of ruin if he wins about the same amount as he loses every time. It actually is a better probability for your account if you have *fewer* winning trades but hold those winners for a higher profit/loss ratio. Of course, the best of all worlds is to be in the far right side of the matrix. A trader with 60% or more winning trades and only a slightly better profit/loss ratio than 1:1 has *no chance of ruin.*

Something else that is astounding when you think this through is that this calculation is based on only 100 events in a sample set. Flipping a coin and predicting heads versus tails will be a 52% ratio. When the matrix is calculated for a higher sample set, the percent probability goes *down* for a trading system but *remains the same* for flipping coins. That means that if you did 1,000 trades with a 42% winning trade ratio and a 2:1 profit/loss ratio, the probability drops to less than 8%. The more consistent you are the better you do, even if your ability to pick winning trades is less than chance. This is where "black box" or systems traders have their success levels. They really are not in the business of picking winning trades; they are in the business of *holding winners* and remaining completely consistent in how they select trades.

In order to exploit the probability of ruin matrix for your personal trading you need to know where you fall to begin with. I would suggest you go back and review the last 100 trades you did and calculate your ratios. Once you have that knowledge, you can begin to develop changes to your approach in order to exploit your trading strengths and minimize your trading weaknesses. If you discover that you have a high ratio of winning trades to losing trades, you simply need to develop the skill of holding your winners longer. Perhaps that means waiting 24 more hours before liquidating. Maybe you have a low percentage of winners but you are regularly taking two or three dollars out for every one lost. This could indicate that you need to improve your entry timing a bit. Sometimes it means you are running your initial protective stop-loss order too close to your entry; maybe a wider stop will help you find a winner a bit better. Of course, the flip side to that is you will need to trade a smaller position, but you get the idea.

The information you compile from your record keeping can provide you with all sorts of information to improve these ratios. One trader I worked with discovered that he had a very high percentage of winning trades to losing trades on Monday through Wednesday each week but that his ratio dropped on Thursday and Friday. He made a new rule for himself: If he was not up by a certain amount of profit by Wednesday afternoon, he would quit for the week. If his equity dropped at all on a Thursday or a Friday, he would not give back more than a certain percent of his Monday through Wednesday profits. He really never improved any other part of his approach with that knowledge. He simply discovered that he was great to start the week but he had a tendency for losses later in the week. Armed with knowledge of his personal trade performance, he improved his ratios to the far right of the matrix.

If you think about being in any business there is a correlation between success and the information available. Some businesses are closed on weekends. They have learned from experience that Saturdays and Sundays cost more than they bring in. Other businesses don't need a storefront. Every business has parts that can be improved and things that need to be done more often to increase the success potential.

In the trading environment, there are parts of what we do every day that will not put money in our trading account. There are things that will put money into our account easily and things that increase the potential that money will go away. By keeping very detailed and accurate records of your *actual performance*, you can calculate how well you are doing net. You need to know what you are really doing well and what needs to be improved. Because trading is what it is and a certain amount of our net results is not in our control, we need data about our net results to help us change what *is* in our control. Knowing our ratios will keep us on track and show us where we need to develop additional controls on our behavior.

Always remember, the winning numbers are 42% won/loss ratio and a 2:1 profit/loss ratio. I also recommend including your commissions and fees in your profit/loss ratio. They are part of your expense picture, so you need to account for them.

Know When to Take a Break

When things are at their darkest, pal, it's a brave man that can kick back and party.
—Dennis Quaid, as Lt. Tuck Pendleton in *Innerspace*

One of the hardest things for new traders to do is to appreciate that the markets aren't going anywhere. The worldwide evolution of financial markets is just like the evolutionary process evident in any growth. Biological life-forms mutate and change, weather patterns develop and change, technology develops and replaces older technology; anything where you can find some sort of a growth pattern will most likely continue to develop and change. I think it is a safe bet that the current business and economic climate will be included in that process of change and development. What is almost certain is that financial markets won't take a step backward or cease to exist. The markets aren't going anywhere.

Most traders would agree with this point of view, but that is where they stop. It is easy to say that we know the markets will be here tomorrow and most likely for as long as humans live here, but it is quite another to remove yourself from the trading environment and simply go do something else for a while. Many traders have a hard time doing that. Most traders feel a tremendous sense of loss if they are unable to remain connected to the market almost continually; they don't want to miss that critical piece of news or that perfect trade. Many traders will literally stay awake for days at a time, trading as close to 24 hours around the clock as

117

they can. If the particular market they trade is closed until the next day, these traders feel compelled to analyze their positions, select multiple opportunities for the next trading session, or pore endlessly over market commentary.

As a group, traders have an almost manic obsession with their market and the profit potential they perceive to be available every day. For these individuals to stop trading, even for just one day, is a huge challenge. Just look at the proliferation of portable, handheld trading interfaces offering real-time execution. What opportunity could be so grossly overwhelming that I can't afford to ride the bus for 15 minutes because I might lose a profit?

All of this voluminous market data and all of the state-of-the-art trading vehicles have evolved over time as a method of either making sense of the madness or exploiting an ever more esoteric opportunity related to the underlying fact that *everything is changing and it will never stop*. If you want to, you can trade options on options, you can trade pollution futures, you can trade electricity, and you can trade indexes on indexes; plus you can get real-time data on a palm computer while you are riding in a cab on the way to your daughter's recital. Don't forget your cell phone in case you have to call one of your many brokers and get your fills on your trades done in Asia or Europe last night (or was it this morning?).

This is insanity.

None of this super-connectivity or mobility will ever help any trader make better trades or maximize his potential. I want to remind everyone that the current state of evolution and financial specialization has not improved the trading environment enough to make more losers into winners and more winners into bigger winners. Financial evolution is spinning out of control as we start the twenty-first century.

We need to remember that trading is not a science—it is an art form. Science does not make good art; that is why it is science. As a trader who wants to develop and maintain his edge for optimal performance and maximum profits, you would be wise to take a step back and focus on what it is that really creates your profits. Your *thinking* creates your opportunities, and if your thinking suffers, so does your opportunity.

I am of the opinion that trading is an intensely personal and subjective experience. No two traders will ever see the market in exactly the same way. No two traders will ever position themselves exactly the same way. No two traders will focus on the same information in exactly the same way, and no two traders will ever come to the same conclusion about price action. The only thing any two traders have in common is the fact that they buy and sell in the same place. It is because of this personal and subjective nature of the trading environment that the issue of knowing when to take a break is so crucial. The moment your thinking stops being your best thinking possible, your performance starts to slip.

If you observe any top performer in any field, you will probably notice a few things. First, they play their game their way. If they are in business, for example, they do things a certain way and they seldom move too far away from that baseline activity. If they do change something they are doing in a particular way, they will have a very sound, well-thought-out reason. Next, they know what is important to make a profit and guard that potential in as many ways as possible. It really doesn't matter what the profit potential is or how it is realized, they know what will work and they know that they know. As traders, we do the same things.

But many top performers in other fields remember one more thing. They see life as a whole. They are interested in *balance*. They know that life is made up of many different things and that business is just one of them. In fact, they will tell you the reason they are in business the way they are is to enjoy the various other parts of life more completely, and that those things create more energy for them to work better. Business is more of a means than an end for those top performers. If you look at the lives of top-performing athletes, you will notice that while some things are different, there is a baseline that is very similar. They train regularly to stay in physical condition, they are disciplined about things like what they eat or drink, they practice their game to stay on edge, and, most important, *they know when to rest.*

In almost any other profession there is a range of performance across all participants. Not everyone in a profession is a top performer, but in most professions you can earn a paycheck without being a top performer. In trading, if you are not a top performer, you most likely will suffer losses. It is wise to remember that you are not competing against other traders. You are competing against yourself. If you are not at the top of your game when you play, the probability that you will beat yourself increases.

Due to the subjective and personal nature of trading, part of a strong daily market presence must include proper rest. By that I don't mean just a good night's sleep, although that goes without saying. I mean you should take time to recharge your mental batteries. Only you can determine what that means for you personally, but you need to make regular time to get away from the markets and rest. While you are doing whatever it is that works for you, consider maybe that would also include no access to the markets as well. Perhaps part of your trade plan would be a regular weekly, monthly, or quarterly time for something else, and that includes leaving your laptop at home.

For me personally, I discovered that regular time away from the markets allowed me to relax and take a fresh perspective on things. I usually include a long four-day weekend every two or three months. If I have been doing well enough I might make it an out-of-town trip, but I always take a few days to recharge. I have a lot of hobbies that I try to enjoy more often, like building model airplanes. All of these little and larger ways of getting away from the markets does one very important thing: It frees my thinking and preserves a sense of balance. I discovered that trading, although very exciting and interesting, cannot be done to my optimum performance if I am not properly balanced. There is more to life than what we do for a living, no matter where we fall on the scale of success.

If you have a spouse or children, a sense of balance is even more critical. Many marriages have suffered when one spouse or the other gets so involved with what they do to earn income that there is no time or energy to care for what really matters—our relationships, family, and physical health. Don't be one of those traders who climb the ladder of success only to find that it was leaning against the wrong wall. Show respect for your personal state of mind and the emotional health of those around you by properly balancing the intense world of successful trading with the infinitely more valuable world of people and personal health. No truly successful person will allow his life to fall out of balance. Trading can require more creativity, passion, commitment, and energy than most professions; trading also has the potential to leave nothing left at the end of the day for anything else. Part of a well-rounded market presence is doing something regularly that preserves your sense of balance.

Daily exercise is a great way to keep your sense of balance. Taking at least one day on the weekend to do something that requires little or no thinking is another great way to remain balanced—something like taking the kids to the zoo or a ball game. Planning a vacation at least once a year for more than just a day or two is another great way to recharge. Personally, I take the last two weeks of the year off for the holidays. Anything related to the markets I leave at the office and I head to the islands to do some sailing. I come back completely recharged and ready to tackle the next year's opportunities.

I'm not saying that these things will work for you, but there are doubtless things that you personally enjoy very much that are often excluded from your life due to the pressures of trading. Doing those things regularly while disconnecting from the markets will help keep your head clear. You won't be run down, tired, lacking energy, burned out, or juggling too many balls in the air when the right opportunity comes along. Also, you will have the mental resources free to manage those trades better, and you will see more of them.

The important thing to remember is that this rule is about *improving your performance*. You really don't need to trade every day. You aren't going to miss anything. The markets will never end and they will be here when you are back from getting tuned up again. You aren't going to miss anything so spectacular that a game of tennis will ruin your whole year. When you feel your performance start to slip a bit, take some time to step back, turn off the noise, and get balanced again.

The trader who tries to do it all, all the time, is the one who will make a mistake. Don't be that trader. Know when to take a break.

Don't Trade the News

A danger foreseen is half avoided.
—Thomas Fuller, *Forbes Thoughts on Opportunity*

O ne of the more interesting phenomena related to price action is the relationship between news (fundamentals) and a trader's participation. There is an old trader saying that you must have heard at one point: "Buy the rumor, sell the fact." This rule developed from observations made by traders over the years, and it has evolved into a more complex kind of timing tool that I call "Don't trade the news."

The psychology behind this rule is not very complex at all. Nor is this rule supposed to encourage traders to ignore fundamentals. Rather, there is a unique relationship between *news* and *timing* that makes participating in the market *because* of the news very deadly to your equity. Stop again and think through the issue of net order flow, open trades, and traders who want to get into or out of a position. Remember also that not everyone in the market can have a profit, due to the nature of zero-sum trading. As we discussed before, you *cannot* profit unless you are on the right side of the net order flow. Why does anyone open a position? Because they expect to make money from a *perception* they have about price potential. When the perception is acted on, the trader executes. When learning to use this rule, it is this *perception* that is our concern.

Let's use a very simple illustration to see the value of this rule. Let's suppose it is early October of the year and the orange juice crop is about to be harvested. October happens to be the height of the hurricane season as well. On Monday of this hypothetical first week, weather forecasters alert the media that out in the mid-Atlantic Ocean a tropical depression is brewing into a hurricane. The expected path of this hurricane includes the potential for a direct pass over the heart of the Florida Peninsula—directly through the center of the orange belt, where two-thirds of the U.S. consumption is grown. Orange juice futures begin to climb in price as traders speculate that the hurricane might severely damage the orange belt or even destroy this year's crop. Some traders wait to see how this develops.

As Monday turns into Tuesday, then Wednesday, it becomes more and more certain that by Saturday morning, this hurricane will come ashore as a Category 5 storm *right down the center of the orange belt.* Orange juice futures continue to climb. On Thursday the weather center declares there is a 95% chance that this storm will pass through the orange belt. By the closing bell on Friday, orange juice futures are locked limit up and, to make matters worse, the market won't open for two days—not until after the hurricane has blown away the orange crop on Saturday morning. The pool of unfilled buy orders continues to grow until the end of the day as speculators try to get in on what is a certain higher potential for the following week.

A seasoned trader knows exactly how this plays out, but let's just fast-forward to Monday's open. As the news reports come in from the Florida orange belt Saturday night and Sunday morning, the devastation is just tremendous. Not only have people lost their homes, businesses, even loved ones, but the orange belt is estimated to have lost at least half of this year's crop. As soon as the phones are open on Monday morning, the pool of buy orders continues to grow with traders just absolutely certain that they won't see another glass of orange juice on their kitchen table for months. The market is called limit up on the open.

The bell is rung and yes, the market opens limit up, but then starts trading. It takes about an hour, but by that time the pool of market orders on the buy side has been absorbed by the willing sellers. Slowly the market starts to quietly tick lower. Suddenly the market breaks. By the end of the day, the orange juice market is locked limit down and the Monday buyers can't get out of their longs. The market is called limit down on the open Tuesday.

What happened? After all, *the orange juice crop is gone!*

But that's not the point. The point is that people were trading the news—or rather their *perception* of the news. The even better question is, who were the willing sellers?

The willing sellers are the same buyers who bought the market on Monday a week ago. They bought the rumor. By the time the rumor became a fact, the move had already happened and, *in fact,* it was the higher price action *before* the actual fundamental event that convinced the late buyer to buy. His *perception* was that orange juice was headed even higher and he waited until he was *absolutely certain*. The professional trader was following the rule; the amateur trader was *trading the news*.

It is important to note that traders are smarter now than they were 20 years ago, technical analysis is more sophisticated, and trader knowledge is greater. Even the most novice trader today has access to information and trade help that professional pit traders didn't have 20 years ago. The markets get smarter every year. Most novice traders know or have heard the rule "Buy the rumor, sell the fact." The difficulty is in separating rumor from fact—knowing what fundamental is being closely watched by the market this week and how susceptible that market is to unexpected news causing a panic.

In my view, the kind of situation described in this hypothetical orange juice market probably has gone the way of the dinosaur. Most markets wouldn't react in that way to most of the unexpected fundamentals that might drive trader perception. The point is that *news* and the *perception of news* are what create some traders' urge to action. When the news is released, these traders form an opinion as to what the news means—they decided it is either bullish or bearish, *right now* for them personally. They then execute and, more often than not, their open position is on the wrong side of the net order flow.

The maxim "Don't trade the news" is about waiting until the panic/perception of less-informed/less-skilled traders have placed themselves at risk. The unskilled trader makes that choice because he has formed an equal relationship in his mind between *fundamentals* and *prices*. This trader believes that the prices will advance or decline *because* of something. The major element missing in this thinking is, of course, the relationship between net order flow and a losing position. If a trader places himself on the wrong side of the net order flow, the reason for being there is not a critical part of the trade. The reason used by the individual trader to get in a market has little or nothing to do with that market's true potential to move.

The problem with trading *because* of the news is that by the time a fundamental news item is released, traders have already positioned themselves, and the winning traders have only done that from their understanding of the net order flow. If, for example, the news is bullish, the winning trader who is already long liquidates his long by selling to the new trader who is initiating a long *because* of the news. The bullish potential created by the news is absorbed by the trader liquidating into the news. This is why any fundamental news release is almost always followed by at least some opposite trade pressure shortly thereafter. In this illustration, the market has now run out of buyers. As the longs from under the market continue to liquidate and/or new sellers come in, they are competing for a smaller group of fewer and fewer new buyers. Once those late buyers are in, the market has nowhere to go but lower. The market has gone south on a bullish piece of news.

This potential is always there and is almost always certain if the news is a regular report or a weekly release of some kind. There is more of a chance that better-informed traders will open positions prior to the release, and that once the news is actually released, the remaining traders who execute *because* of that news are used by the winners to liquidate their winning positions.

Obviously, trading is not that cut-and-dried. There are times when markets don't move countertrend on the news, unexpected things cause people to panic, or a market breaks out huge on a news story. I am not suggesting that you should fade the news when you trade. I am suggesting that a market is more indefinable just ahead of and just after a fundamental news event, expected or not. Your best course of action to reduce your risk exposure is to not trade the news.

I find that the best way to help define market price action when the news is actively influencing traders is to remember a few basic things. First, if you don't have a lead on the market, don't trade ahead of the news or after the news for at least one hour. Give things time to settle down a bit. Ahead of the news, the price range will be very tight anyway, and after the news the initial rush of panicky traders will be washed out. Two-sided violent trade is usually the case for the first hour or so after news is released. If the market runs away in one direction, and it was the direction you wanted, you will just have to wait for the pullback that is certain to come. Don't chase the market. You won't be perfectly positioned in any market anyway. Let things settle down before acting so you are not the trader getting whipsawed.

Second, the news is always factored in. No matter what the report, news, or economic numbers may be when released, every trader has already decided what it means for them and how they will behave. Every trader has decided that if the news is one thing, they will do such-and-such; if the news is another thing, they will do something else. Some traders are in already with a lead, and if the news is such-and-such they will liquidate; if it is something else, they will add to the position. All news, numbers, or reports are already in the market.

Last, the news can only be one of three things. The news, reports, or numbers can only be

1. As expected
2. Better than expected
3. Worse than expected

Once the news is out, traders will behave not according to the news, but according to their *perception* that the news was either better than, worse than, or as expected. Once they execute from that perception, the market has order flow. How the market behaves with that order flow is a clue to the market's *real* nature, not the market's *expected* nature.

As an example, if a piece of news is due Thursday, is forecast to be bullish, and prices have advanced higher since Monday, but the actual news released is worse than expected (bearish), whatever the market does next is a great clue moving forward. If the market just takes off higher, what does that tell you? If the market just sits there, what does that tell you? If the market breaks hard but rallies back in 20 minutes, what does that tell you?

The point is simply that observing the market's *actual behavior* post-news gives the clearest indication of how traders are currently positioned, how nervous or confident they might be, and how willing they are to execute. The one constant is that the trader who is making his choice to execute in or out of the market, and basing that choice *on the news itself* and not on the net order flow, is usually in the wrong spot. Don't trade alongside that poorly positioned trader. Let him get out of the way first.

Don't
Take Tips

*Tips! How people want tips! They crave not only to
get them but to give them. There is greed involved,
and vanity. It is very amusing, at times, to watch
really intelligent people fish for them. And the tip-
giver need not hesitate about the quality, for the
tip-seeker is not really after good tips, but after
any tip.*

— Edwin Lefèvre, *Reminiscences of
a Stock Operator*

O ne of my earliest trading experiences involved taking a tip. It
was the early 1980s, and the tip was to buy silver and this was
the early 1980s. If you have no knowledge of the attempted
corner in the silver market by the Hunt Brothers, I would suggest you
take a few extra minutes when you have time and look up the details;
it is a fascinating story. For me personally it is more than a fascinating
story because somewhere in the world, there is someone who has
my $500.

I was a sophomore in college and I had a few bucks saved. I was sitting in class before the bell and one of my classmates was extolling the
profit potential in the silver market. As it turns out, he was from a family
on the wealthier side and apparently his father had made a killing in the
silver market. Maybe it was silver that was paying his tuition. I decided to
head over to the local jewelry store and ask about buying some silver. I
carried $500 worth of silver bullion home one afternoon. That silver lost
80% of its value within a year.

I didn't consider it a trade; I was not a trader at that point. I had no idea how investments, trading, or the markets worked yet. I simply bought into the story that silver was going to trade higher. I never thought for a moment about what creates prices, who told me the data, or whether it was true. I just listened to the common sense of the argument and went with it.

The whole experience became part of the catalyst to become a trader when I learned about silver futures. I discovered someone could be *short*. As my silver bullion declined in value, someone else was getting rich. *Wow!*

When we choose to listen to a tipster, the problem is not the information. The problem is not the quality of the stock or commodity market. The problem is not even whether the tip is wrong. The problem is within us as traders. When we fail to do our own homework and let someone else's thinking become our guide, our results will never be any better than the thinking of the tipster. It doesn't matter if the tip is a winner or how persuasive the tipster is. When we let someone else do our thinking for us, we run the risk that the quality of that thinking is nowhere near accurate for the market in question. The problem is in failing to think—not in the tip.

No matter how you choose to participate in the markets, you are ultimately responsible. When you finally decide that *now* is the time to execute, it is your money at risk. If you have a gain or a loss, the credit or debit is assigned to *your* account, no one else's. Why would you let someone else determine your results?

The problem with tips is not the data, because that data is really the same for any point of view. No matter what conclusion you come to, there will always be another point of view that is created from the exact same set of data. If you and I both compile all the data available in the meat complex and compare it to the technical picture the charts have at that moment, you may come to a bearish conclusion while I come to a bullish conclusion. The important thing is that *neither conclusion matters to make a profit*. The only thing that matters is being on the right side of the net order flow. If your analysis helps you come to a conclusion and it happens to be the correct side of the order flow, money will flow into your account. If your conclusion is not the correct one, money will leave the account. In either case, putting your account balance at risk without knowing for certain what the potential is for the underlying net order flow is simply reckless. When you take a tip, you are increasing your risk because you are accepting the responsibility for a loss without the corresponding knowledge of the market's underlying potential. Taking a tip is really just gambling with your money.

If you think about it, any analysis or market data that you make available for your use is actually a sort of tip. When you use a technical indicator like MACD, for instance, you are placing your equity under the thinking process of Howard Abell, the developer of the MACD indicator. Personally, I like Howard. I have attended his workshops and read his books, and I think he is a very sharp guy. But I also know that the MACD indicator is a mathematical formula that Howard developed. Howard knows that formula best and he will most likely be able to use that indicator better than I ever could because I don't understand the thinking behind it like he does. How can I use Howard's brain to trade my money?

If technical analysis is a sort of tip, and whispers overheard in the CBOT men's room are tips, and government reports are tips, and articles in trade journals are tips; where is the *real data* to trade with?

It's inside your head. No matter what you read, study, or absorb, you personally have to choose the time to execute. The moment you pass from thinking for yourself to trusting something outside of yourself, you are taking a tip. If you trust technical or fundamental analysis past a certain point, charts then become a tipster for you. If you compile reams of data and economic fundamentals, crunch those numbers according to some formula, and trade on that data, then government reports are your tipster. If you go to a psychic and ask to see the future waiting ahead in the meat complex, you are definitely taking a tip.

I think we as traders are susceptible to tips because we really would like to believe that there is just *one more piece of data* that will disclose where the winning trade is. We desperately want to feel like we have covered every possible piece of information and haven't left anything out. We have *really* done our homework and no stone was left unturned. Yet so-and-so said . . .

In my view, the psychology behind this rule is really twofold. First, it prevents us from putting ourselves at a needless risk or trading for reasons that are not our own. We need to focus on market structure and trade from a sense of discipline, not gamble and hope someone else is right. Second, we need to constantly remind ourselves that our account balance is ultimately our responsibility and we are fully in control when we execute. Nothing determines our results except our actions, and those actions need to be well thought out, proactive, and in harmony with the market we trade, not based on some mumbo-jumbo we overheard at a bar, read in a book, or created for ourselves by running a computer simulation. Successful trading is a function of several things all working at once, not a result of opinion or conjecture—even if the source of that opinion or conjecture has an impressive set of credentials. A tip is only one point of view. Right or wrong, the problem with the tip is not the data; it is the fact that the choice to assume the risk was not ours.

There is one other thing about tips that I think is critical to keep in mind. As you spend time in the trading arena and become more experienced, there will be times when a trade seems to jump off the screen at you. It is abundantly clear which direction that market has potential in and, better yet, you can see it far enough in advance to *really* hammer the order flow. You are going to make a lot of money on this one and you *know* it.

Then the phone rings and it is one of your trading associates. A conversation starts about various opportunities you both have working and what you see coming down the pipeline. In a very excited voice you begin to extol the virtues of the trade you have just identified. With great confidence you tell your friend exactly what you see coming and why that trade will be one of the home runs this year. After you finish your dissertation your friend is silent for a moment, and then you hear a voice with more confidence than your own speak: "You are nuts! That market is dead. I saw a report on CNBC last month about that entire industry. You might as well stand in the street tearing up $100 bills—you will have more fun." You are stunned but still confident, and you restate your argument; after another 15-minute heated debate you both hang up.

Now you are in trouble, because the trade that appeared to be so certain to you 20 minutes ago is in question. Your friend raised some good points. He is not going to take the trade even though he asked what you saw coming. Basically, because you offered someone a tip when asked, you opened your mind up to an argument about the quality of the tip. You had to defend and justify your trade conclusion to someone who has no intention of seeing it objectively. The emotional tug-of-war leaves you a bit drained and wondering if, God forbid, six weeks from now that trade won't have worked as the way you expected. You will never hear the end of it. Of course, if you are a really weak trader you might decide to skip that trade entirely after listening to your friend—which is also taking a tip.

The rule "Don't take tips" includes the rule "Don't give tips." The mindset of the tip giver and the tip taker are symbiotic and counterproductive to lasting success. If your goal is to remain a net winning trader, your daily trade strategy must include some form of discipline where you neither give nor receive tips. If you are expecting your analysis to provide you trades today, you had better reevaluate your analysis. If you are looking for something in the daily news to give you the confidence to execute, you had better think through what you are expecting from the news. If someone asks you what you think of a certain market today, shake your head and say, "I have no idea." Give yourself the best possible daily trade presence by reducing and eliminating any tendency to look for or take tips. By doing the same for tip giving, you also improve your mental toughness. You stop the vicious cycle of opinion-versus-opinion conclusion making, which is not trading. Opinion-versus-opinion conclusion making is called the House and the Senate.

Withdraw Equity Regularly

Gold comes quickly to the one who does not hesitate to save one coin in ten.
—First of the *Five Laws of Gold* from the book
The Richest Man in Babylon

In the book *The Richest Man in Babylon*, by George S. Clason (New York: Dutton, 1989), the story is told of how a young man wishing to become rich learns the five laws of gold. All five laws are incredibly wise and simple; I am amazed that people are still poor with this kind of knowledge available. The first law is the cornerstone to wealth accumulation and this one law in and of itself will lead to wealth even if you don't follow the other laws.

In the story, the rich merchant teaching the young man tells how the source or size of a man's income is not important to building wealth; it is only important that a part of that income be regularly set aside and put to work. I can tell you from personal experience that my entire trading changed for the better when I applied this rule to my trading accounts. There is something about obeying the tried-and-true laws of wealth and money that make the issue of trading as the source of wealth less important.

You might get rich from trading, but you don't have to if you follow certain timeless principles while you earn profits of any size from your trading. It is a mistake to think that because the markets have unlimited profit potential *you personally* will accumulate unlimited profits. It is better to accept the possibility that you will earn a very nice income or a nice piece of the pie; but what you do with the accumulated profits you have achieved is much more significant for your overall success.

Rather than spend a lot of time on the basics of wealth accumulation, I am going to assume that your intention with this book is to get a better edge for your trading. Part of that edge is creating trading rules that will work for you. If you look closely at the underlying psychology behind winning trading rules, there is a subtle, implied consciousness that they all seem to point to. That consciousness is *nonattachment*. All winning traders have as part of their market presence or daily discipline an awakened knowledge that pretty much anything can happen at any moment. If that results in an adverse move to their market position, they will ruthlessly liquidate. If something unexpected happens that pushes a trade further in profits, they might aggressively add to the position. When a trade is not performing as anticipated, they will liquidate or lighten up. Basically, most winning traders are *not attached* to any particular result, price area, profit/loss ratio, or even any one market. Winning traders know that anything can and does happen, and that if they have any kind of internal commitment to any part of the trading experience they have a higher probability of losing money. That nonattachment extends to their account balance, and this is why regular withdrawals from your account are a very healthy thing for your trading.

This rule is about maintaining a strong market presence. A strong market presence should be thought of as a whole picture. There are a lot of things that can affect trading, and many of those things are not directly related to the markets themselves. For example, if you have a conflict with your spouse and your emotions are in turmoil, it is very likely that you would incur a loss if you initiated a new position. Something from the outside world is pressing in on your inner world. Stop and think about how people you know have made poor choices when they have been subject to something that upset them. Trading is no different. To maintain a strong market presence you must reduce or eliminate outside pressures, as they might disrupt your thinking or emotions. Included in that picture is the issue of what to do with money earned from trading.

Obviously, you need to be a net winning trader to follow this rule. If you aren't a net winning trader at this point, it is still a good idea to consider removing money from your account from time to time. Money is a vital and necessary part of our day-to-day lives, and as such, it should be moved around occasionally as our world changes. The surest way to go broke is to put your money in one place and leave it there forever. Money needs to be used to be valuable. Opportunities change, people change, things that were great investments in the past are no longer good today; money works hardest for you when you are moving it around to take advantage of the changes around you.

If you take the point of view that most winning traders do, you will find your trading improves when your trading plan includes withdrawing funds on a regular basis. You really don't need a huge chunk of money in your trading account to exploit market inequalities. Most of us can focus on only so many markets at one time anyway, so having gains pile up and just sit there is pointless. I know that many traders take the point of view that more cash in their account means they can trade larger. You might be surprised to learn that most long-term successful traders don't load up. Most successful traders are very careful about increasing their base trading size. Instead, when their account balance reaches a certain number, they simply withdraw their gains. Most do it as a measure of self-protection; they worked very hard for those gains and don't want to risk giving it back.

These traders also know, usually from past experience, that increasing their trade size has resulted in a larger ebb and flow to their balance. Many simply can't emotionally negotiate that big of a changing balance day-to-day. These traders are content to trade a certain size and do it very well. Withdrawing money regularly prevents the temptation to change something that is obviously working for them.

Additionally, what are we doing this for, anyway? Isn't the whole point of trading to get rich? I know it is for me. I think whatever trading represents for you personally, somewhere in that point of view is the issue of *what to do with the money*. Many traders make the mistake of having no real financial goal to work toward. Goal setting is an important method to monitor actual progress on improving your personal financial position. Assuming you have some financial goals you are working toward, don't make the mistake of thinking you will attain them all at once when your trading balance reaches a certain point. It is wiser to break those goals down into mileposts and make a contribution toward them on a regular basis as your trading account grows.

For example, I have a friend who withdraws a certain amount of his gains every quarter and puts them in bank certificates of deposit. He doesn't care about the interest that is paid; he does this so that he can't get his hands on the money easily or lose it quickly from overtrading (which he has a tendency to do). He lives in a modest apartment and he is looking to put 50% down on a condominium. This particular trader has blown out more than once, and his rules now include, "Once I have a certain gain, it goes in the bank toward owning a home." When this trader withdraws money, he is validating his sense of purpose and progress. He feels good about working toward financial independence and security as he defines it. He is happier and more focused, which leads to a better market presence. Better market presence, better trade results—they go hand in hand.

Withdrawing money and putting it somewhere is only part of the story. I think you will maintain a much better market focus if you also take

a portion of your gains and do something that is personally very reward-
ing for you. When we as traders have invested a year of our lives and
maintained a sharp edge during that time, sacrificed things to make a nice
profit over time, we owe it to ourselves to reward ourselves in some way
that is deeply satisfying. There is a very powerful sense of satisfaction that
comes when we stop to enjoy the fruits of our labors and invest in our personal happiness. I don't think it really matters what form this takes, just
that we do it for ourselves regularly.

I think this needs to be done no matter what level you are at in your
trader development. If you are trading a $2,000 balance and earn a $500
gain during the quarter, I think you should take $100 and buy yourself din-
ner or something. I think it is crucial for us as traders to invest back into
ourselves when we are achieving the success we have; God knows we
have earned it. Trading can be a brutal experience, and when we are on
the winning side, we should enjoy that success a bit. Of course, it should
go without saying that spending every dollar earned from the markets is
not a good idea. You need to find a balance between enjoying your success
and saving.

In the final analysis, the rule "Withdraw equity regularly" is about the
process of non-attachment to the markets. It is a daily battle for many of
us to hold rather loosely to our trades and their results. When you hold
loosely to your account balance as well, I think you are completing the big
picture of what the markets ultimately mean to you personally. How you
choose to define *financial freedom* is up to you. For me, just knowing that
I have complete control of my finances and I don't answer to anyone is a
huge part of it. I really don't care anymore about material things like I
used to. I take money from my accounts regularly and make secure investments, I support a few charities, and I enjoy a lot of fun stuff. To me that is
freedom. I don't think I could maintain that sense of freedom or daily balance if I had a huge cash balance in my trading accounts going back to the
day I started. What good does that do?

Your trading results when they are cash credits must mean something
to you personally. Take that cash and use it; move it around and increase
your opportunity base. Make a few long-term secure investments, buy a
vacation home, take your spouse to Europe for a month; do something
positive with those gains and you will be a sharper trader for it.

Be a Contrarian

Buy when there is blood in the streets . . .

—J. P. Morgan

E very trader has most likely had the experience of planning out a trade, waiting for the point he feels is the right price/time relationship, executing, and then seeing the market go the other way almost instantly. In maybe only a few seconds the market has taken a large chunk of equity away. If this has happened to you, you know the feeling of confusion and sometimes anger that results—all that preparation and work gone out the window.

Many traders attempt to analyze the result and look for a way they could have seen that situation coming ahead of time. Other traders try to figure out how they could have seen the other side and put the opposite trade out instead of their first choice. In my view, all of these responses to the result are leading to worse trader performance. Analysis of the market can only go so far to begin with and the fact is, the loss most likely came because you were following the crowd. True, you may not have known you were following the crowd at the time but that is what contrary thinking is all about.

Many fine books have been written on crowd behavior. I have included a few titles in the Recommended Reading section of this book. I don't think we need to go deeply into the psychology of crowds in this short rule, but I do think it is worth noting that all markets are crowds. As a trader looking to build a strong market presence, you really don't need to become an expert on crowd behavior. You only need to know what the crowd behavior is most likely to be at some point.

What motivates the crowd? I have spent a lot of time getting my thinking around the concept of markets as a crowd, and I think I can say with some certainty that a market is in reality nothing more than an expression of three basic emotions: fear, greed, and hope. The other things that traders feel compelled to focus on as a support system to create confidence all boil down to a reason to hope, a reason to get paid, and a reason to pursue a profit with less fear. But the underlying emotional structure of the market is based on the need to avoid pain and the desire to make money. This is why traders are tempted to hope a market comes back when they are holding losses, why they hope a market continues further their way, why they get out if the market starts taking away an open-trade profit, why they hesitate to do the right thing at the right time, and all the other various behaviors that increase probabilities of net losses. The bottom line to all of this is *trader behavior*, and that behavior is driven by these three emotions.

Net winning traders still have these emotions, but they have one thing the losing trader does not: a deeper understanding of the crowd they participate in. Net winning traders also know that their behavior must be different from the crowd's behavior. This difference in behavior is the essential part of contrary thinking.

Almost all winning traders have controls on their behavior. That is what this book is really all about: giving traders a clearer understanding of where they need to focus their thinking and behavior. Creating your personal daily trade rules comes from an adequate understanding of the psychology you need in order to achieve net winning performance. Net winning traders experience all the same emotions as losing traders, but their behavior controls prevent those emotions from becoming *losing behaviors*. One of the absolute best controls you can develop is the propensity to *stop thinking like the market crowd to begin with*.

Most discussions of contrary thinking seem to focus more on learning to be bullish when the market is bearish, or vice versa. Actually, that is a useful tool, but I am not going to have that discussion. I am suggesting that contrary thinking is more about understanding that the crowd is thinking along certain lines and you need to think along a different line. Sometimes that means you need to be looking at the bullish scenario when the market is declining; sometimes it means you need to fade the news; sometimes you need to stay away for a time.

The crowd behavior will almost always be driven by fear, greed, and hope, and those emotions are stimulated in the crowd by price action or the absence of price action. Remember, the prices *mean* something to each participant. When that meaning becomes an urge to action, a trade results. For example, if a market is declining against someone's open long, that *means* a trader is losing money. He wants to avoid that pain, so he will either hope the market reverses or get out if he fears a further price decline. Once that urge gets strong enough, the trader will liquidate. What does that kind of behavior look like in the actual market price action?

In your day-to-day analysis of the market, you would do better if you listened closely to the personal *meanings* you associate with price action. For example, most traders tend to use the word *strong* to attach meaning to a market rising in price. *Weak* describes a declining market. Now, if you look closely at what you are doing when you attach meaning to a price direction, you have more clues as to how other traders, too, are most likely observing price action. In other words, the crowd believes the market is strong when prices are rising. What do you do with a strong market? You buy it, of course; strong is good.

At some point in this strong market the available universe of potential buyers will have come to that same conclusion and have placed themselves at risk. They will have bought a position, correct? Now the market fails to advance. The buyer is afraid the strong market will now weaken and the potential exists for a loss. This fear now drives the buyer to sell, creating a self-fulfilling prophecy. If this whole dance happens with enough participants then the previously strong market now becomes weak and prices decline. The buyer has a loss—but the seller who let him in is the winner.

To be that winning seller is not as simple as being bearish when everybody is bullish; it's more a process of knowing enough about average emotional thinking and how that will stimulate someone to do something. In the markets, you are looking for the point where that has already happened. When the market has run out of buyers, it is physically impossible for that market to continue to advance—all the force that could be exerted on the buy side has already happened. All it takes is one seller to start the ball rolling the other way.

But in either case, the market is neither strong nor weak; it is simply a machine, processing orders in one direction or the other. What you are attempting to do is take advantage of the changing net order flow. That net order flow is created by the actions of each crowd participant. As each crowd participant comes to a conclusion and executes, the market is preset to go the other way sooner or later under some time frame; those initiating orders must eventually be offset with a liquidating order from the other side. Contrary thinking is about understanding that the crowd is doing one thing from the net perspective every day and that they will have to do the other thing eventually, maybe in a time frame you can see right now. In other words, once everybody has entered the market, they must leave the market sooner or later. You as a successful trader are attempting to be *just ahead* of that change in the net order flow; most likely that will mean a buy order when everyone is selling, or a sell order when everyone is buying. Contrary thinking is about being in the right place at the right time to exploit the crowd thinking.

It is important to remember that most people can come to a conclusion that is fairly accurate. Accurate thinking is not the same thing as accurate behavior. Many traders with only average understanding of fundamental and technical considerations can call a market. I am sure that you personally have come to the conclusion that a market was bullish or bearish, and that conclusion proved over time to be the right one. Calling a market is not the hard part, in my opinion; the hard part is buying or selling at the best times to capture the move. I am certain that some of my readers have been 100% correct on a market but didn't make the potential gain for their account, or even had losses. The issue there is not the understanding of market potential; it is the lack of understanding regarding crowd behavior.

Most traders are not very skilled in reading the crowd well enough to know *when* the market is due to move the other way against the mostly right market call. In other words, wait for the correction or confirmation before entering the position; and that is often at the point when the early trader is liquidating with an early loss. Just knowing the underlying market potential is not enough to get in a winning position. You must also think differently about the same conclusion the average market participant has come to. If everyone is bullish and the market is indeed rising, everyone is thinking the same thing: Get long, buy a pullback. But there will be a certain percent of bullish traders who will be washed out on that correction for various reasons and actually have a loss, even though they were right about the market. You want to be a buyer from those traders when they sell off their poorly set longs.

Knowing that potential going in every day is how you exploit the crowd's behavior, and *that* is contrary thinking. Contrary thinking is not coming to a conclusion that is different from other traders. It is not being bullish when everyone is bearish. Contrary thinking is about understanding the game so well that you know when it is time to go against the crowd. Your thinking process starts in a different place and you are not looking to be a bull or a bear in any market. You are attempting to outthink a crowd that does very little thinking in the first place. Sometimes that means you buy an upside breakout because you know the short has his stops up there; sometimes you sell into a rally because you know the crowd is buying the news; sometimes you stand aside because you know the bulls and bears are whipsawing themselves and you need to let the dust settle. Contrary thinking is more about thinking *beyond* emotional behavior, and then having the courage to exploit it without making the same mistake the crowd is making. In other words, you execute against the crowd when the time is right, and then you don't panic, scare yourself out, cut a profit short, or hope the market comes back if you are losing. You control your actions fully by discipline, but those actions come from a completely other kind of confidence.

All Markets Are Bearish

Psssssttt . . . want to know a secret? There is no such thing as a bull market!
—Attributed to Jesse Livermore, 1921, a raging bear

Knowledge is power. In the trading environment there are different kinds of knowledge, and some knowledge is more powerful than others. The most powerful kind of knowledge remains knowing the net order flow; everything else is more along the lines of helpful information.

During the process of gaining the knowledge I needed in order to know which knowledge is really useful, I had to make a lot of observations. Those observations were of people, people's behavior, trade fundamentals, technical study, and general market conditions. Over the years, I have seen a lot of strange things as a full-time trader. I suppose there are hundreds of stories I could tell you about blowouts, blunders, quick fortunes made or lost, unbelievable risks taken or ignored—all sorts of things. I have had my share of wild rides, and as any seasoned trader can tell you, any trader's results are 100% personal. We create them and no one else is responsible for them. We hope for consistent positive results, but until we discover our personal winning trade method, we will have losses.

As we get more educated, as we get *the knowledge we need*, we discover how many of our losses were avoidable. As the stories that are our personal trade results get created, and as we develop better skill, we realize how many of our negative results are self-created. There are countless different ways to lose money. Of course, the absolute worst kind of loss is the one where we simply did not do our homework. For whatever reason, we chose a trade, executed, and had a loss, but that loss was completely avoidable. If we had just known what we needed to know, we might have avoided that loss.

Part of getting that practical kind of knowledge is a very firm understanding of *basic market structure*. Basic market structure is like a playing field. To use a sports illustration, a football field is where the game is played. The game is dynamic and subject to rules that both sides must play by, but the playing field itself provides the basic structure.

One of the most important pieces of information you can possess as part of your trading knowledge is the fact that bull markets are aberrations. All markets are inherently bearish. If you want to reduce the number of trade conclusions you come to that are losing conclusions, you need to understand that coming to a bullish conclusion needs a lot of support. A bullish conclusion has a certain degree of extra risk. You would do better over the life of your trading if you started each hypothesis from the point of view that the market in question will be under net selling pressure in most cases. A bullish market conclusion or trade hypothesis needs a tremendous amount of verification and support because in most cases the bullish potential cannot overcome net selling pressure long enough for a consistent bull market to develop. Just knowing that all markets are bearish will save you a lot of time and money, because there will never be as many quality long trades as there are short trades. You will prevent a lot of needless losses in your account when you are suspicious of bullish conclusions in the first place.

I need to make sure we are all on the same page as far as an understanding of the maxim "All markets are bearish." For the purpose of trading, equities could be excluded from this assumption because equities are not a zero-sum transaction for the most part. I think of equities as a game of musical chairs, whereas futures, options, and FOREX are a tug of war. Equities can pass from one owner to another regardless of whether the share drops in value, pays a dividend, is repurchased by the issuer, gets absorbed by another company, and so on. Equities will often be bought and held for decades. There are a lot of reasons to own equities besides the net change in the share price. A bull market in stocks happens when more money is pumped into the market, not when shorts offset.

The zero-sum transaction market is a completely different animal. Exactly 50% of all contracts traded will be offset at a loss; there is no other way for the market to function. Whoever holds the losing contract has a loss—even in a bull market there will be shorts that cover at a loss and longs that cover at a loss. But there is one important distinction that zero-sum markets have that no other market has: A certain part of the executed trades will never be offset.

For the most part, zero-sum markets are comprised of two separate and distinct participants who have two very different, competing desires. They use the market for vastly different reasons. These two participants are the speculator and the hedger. For the sake of illustration, let's use a simple consumable commodity to document the net bearish nature of the zero-sum market. Every year, a new crop of corn is planted and harvested. Corn is consumed every day and eventually, if no new corn was planted and harvested, we would run out of corn. For the sake of this illustration I want you to set aside all the unique particulars you know about the Corn market. Forget all about the fundamentals, technicals, oscillators or indicators, historical prices of Corn—*everything*. The only thing I want you to focus on is the closed universe of actual executed trades and what that means from a net perspective.

The hedger is the individual who grows Corn and sells it, probably a farmer. The purpose of the Corn futures market—the only reason it exists—is for this farmer to exploit a high price at which he can sell his corn, often before he even grows it. As a farmer, if I am uncertain that the current high price will still be around when it comes time to harvest and sell the crop I plan to grow, I would sell my entire projected crop at the current price of corn futures. If the price of corn goes higher, I can't participate in that additional profit, because I locked up my crop before then, but my benefit is certain: I will have a profit this year. If the opposite happens, such as a big drop in corn prices, I will still have a nice profit this year because I own the right to sell my crop to someone at a higher price—and that contract is guaranteed by the exchange. The buyer of my crop is obligated to pay that price.

The speculator, on the other hand, is looking to exploit price action to make a personal profit due to changes in the price of corn. He probably has never seen an ear of corn except at a barbeque. He has no idea how it is grown or what it is used for besides eating at a barbeque; he spends little time speaking with farmers who produce the corn. He simply compiles the data he finds valuable and decides when it is time for the price to rise or fall. He places himself at risk, and once that happens he will either have a profit or a loss; that is all the speculator cares about. As far as the speculator is concerned, the corn market is nothing more than a potential check in the mailbox.

You are probably saying, "Yeah, I know that—I have been trading for years. What does this have to do with a bear market?"

The point is—in this case—the hedger's selling pressure is never answered with a corresponding buy order. The market has more net sell orders as long as the hedger participates. The hedger *sells* the market. He doesn't have to *buy* the market. He may deliver against his position. Therefore the speculator who buys and sells is the *net force* on the market. Sooner or later that will create a permanent net selling market. To see how, look at Figure 24.1.

Now, suppose the market has apparently become bullish. *Speculators* are buying the market, and the sellers that are letting them in are other *speculators*. The losing speculators on the sell side continue to buy back their losing shorts, creating a price advance due to the net order flow imbalance from the buy side. Prices advance to a point that is considered too high for everybody.

Enter the *hedger*. The hedger sells, the speculative seller opens a new short, and the open trade longs decide to liquidate and they also sell. At this point, that market is under *three times* the selling pressure it normally had been under up to that point. This is why markets always break faster than they rally. Once the winning shorts from above the market decide to cover, that is the only buying pressure left. When those winning shorts cover, the game is over. The losing longs have to sell at a loss and the hedger doesn't have to let them out. The hedgers from above the market don't have to do anything. In fact, a bona fide hedger is not subject to margin requirements or forced liquidation to begin with; once they sell into the market, they really are under no further obligation the way the speculator is. The bull market was a temporary aberration that was exploited by the hedger or professional short-seller. The longs had no chance net, even

Type	Initiation	Liquidation
Short hedger	X	
Short speculator	X	X
Long speculator	X	X
Total force	3	2
Net force =	+ 1 to sell side	

FIGURE 24.1 Forced Liquidation Matrix

though the price advance may have been several months long and many shrewd traders may have pulled some money out.

Obviously, the relationship between the hedger and the speculator is more complex. Hedgers will scale positions into a price rise; they will buy back on breaks in price to confuse participants as well as draw more longs in. Speculators will be long from one area and then short at another area; fundamentals will develop that change the way participants are seeing new price potential. All sorts of things will play out during a temporary bull market. The essential thing to remember is that sooner or later the hedger will have exploited the market from the net sell side and will simply wait for the speculators to exhaust their potential. Once that happens, the remaining net short potential will crush the remaining longs until prices return to a lower equilibrium.

If you want to see historically how bull markets are exploited by professional selling, try looking up the data for the grain bull market in 1988. If you look at the highest prices paid when the rally had become exhaustive, compare that to the Commodity Futures Trading Commission (CFTC) "Commitment of Traders" report. Note the net short position held by hedgers for the two or three weeks leading up to the highs in the grains. The record high open long positions by speculators were all placed into the market during that time as well. There was nowhere for the price to go but lower as those losing longs liquidated and added to the selling momentum. By September of that year prices had fallen back to within a short distance of the ones traded in the spring. The hedgers simply sat on their hands for the most part as prices hit the highs and then declined. By the end of the year, the open trade gains and losses had all been liquidated; delivery notices were not any bigger than usual. Most of the hedgers had covered their shorts, too, probably because the distance in gain was enormous and there was no need to actually deliver the grain against the short contract. The grains have never traded to those highs again since that time, as of this writing in 2006. In fact, due to grain in storage and the import/export situation at the time, there was no real shortage of grain at all, even though some of the crop was lost to the drought that year. There was no bull market. There was a selling opportunity.

I am not trying to oversimplify. I realize that fundamental changes are occurring in the breadth and scope of the marketplace. I know that price action is not as simple as described here, but the important thing is to understand is simply this: Markets exist for the *hedger's benefit*. In most cases, the higher the price goes in any market, the more the hedgers will exploit that from the sell side. Very few markets are used by hedgers from the buy side, and when they do use them, they don't want higher prices either. In both cases, the hedgers really want the buyer to come to the table and play—to assume the risk they don't want. A selling hedger needs the bull market to sell into; he only needs one bull market every few years to hedge several years out. The buying hedger will liquidate his buy hedge at the drop of a hat because it is in his best interests for the price to decline.

Think of it this way: No matter what happens to the fundamental picture, once a bull market develops, the selling hedger will cap that market sooner or later and the buying hedger will sell off his longs once the bull market is over. Both kinds of hedgers need the blood of the speculative bull to return prices to equilibrium after they have protected themselves. By the time the dust settles, in almost all cases, the number of sell orders that have been executed is greater than the number of buy orders; the remaining numbers of open shorts are delivered against. This doesn't have to be a large number of open contracts, only enough to tip the balance to create a no-win situation for the speculative bull who must add pressure from the sell side to take his loss. All three eventual sellers execute, and once prices are lower, the sellers who choose to cover by executing from the buy side will always be fewer than the open shorts who will hold through delivery.

If you are going to trade under bullish conditions, learn to be hyper-vigilant on the activities of hedgers and professional large sellers. They are going to use that bull market to sell into, and when the stage is set, that market is going south in a hurry. Always remember that bull markets are temporary.

Buy/Sell 50% Retracements

You can make a fortune following this one rule alone.
—W.D. Gann, *The Tunnel Through the Air*

Most successful traders will tell you that their systemized approach to executing trades is "very simple" for them. They might appear to be analyzing the market differently than losing traders do, but in reality they are not doing anything different—they are just simplifying the bedrock issue of identifying the net order flow. What they have learned from experience is that certain types of market behavior *look like* the same thing to them every time. From their personal trade results, they know that what looks like the same thing happening is usually followed by a certain higher percentage of price action in a certain direction. In other words, once something happens, and it looks like it is time to buy, since their historical results indicate that they are correct about 67% of the time, they buy. Obviously, the key is in how they are defining what the market "looks like" to them. Most winning traders have a systemized approach that includes a certain amount of basic analysis and discipline, but this "looks like" thing is an intuitive issue.

Developing a winning approach takes time and discipline. You need to keep it simple whenever possible, and you will always do better when you boil down whatever you are learning to the essential teachings contained inside the theory. That is what this rule is about, creating a very simple tool to use successfully. One of the best ways to develop a winning approach, to add that "looks like" component to your personal results, is to enter positions on 50% retracements.

I want to make one thing abundantly clear: 50% retracements are *not* Fibonacci study, projections, or retracements. Fibonacci was a Renaissance mathematician. He was interested in uncovering the grand harmony and design of the universe. He wanted to find the all-pervading, bedrock component to the nature of physical reality—what you and I would call the essence of the physical universe. He lived in a time when money was a very unsophisticated concept. The general level of ignorance in which people existed at the time just before he lived was profound. Fibonacci's discoveries would have been seen as dramatic leaps forward, so much so that they looked like magic and bordered on heresy.

Still, Fibonacci believed things about the nature of reality that you and I know today are completely erroneous. For example, Fibonacci was an alchemist. He believed with all his heart that he would discover, through mathematical design and prayer, the very nature of reality. When he did, he would exploit this knowledge to turn lead into gold, thereby ending his money problems. If I told you that as a trained trader I will trade for you, and that I will execute for your account by studying the flights of bees, you would be no worse off than if you followed Fibonacci through his day as he tried to turn lead into gold.

Fibonacci never applied the golden ratio or the Fibonacci Progression to markets or trading. None of that existed yet. Fibonacci discovered a part of nature that is accurate for the study of nature, nothing else. He didn't know that at the time. He himself lived under a cultural illusion and wasted his knowledge pursuing something that couldn't physically be done.

Why am I telling you this? Because Fibonacci retracement study is an accepted method of simple technical analysis. All successful traders use some form of retracement analysis in their simple methodology. But Fibonacci never intended his discoveries to be developed or applied to trading. That was W. D. Gann's idea, so your best bet in understanding retracements is to study W. D. Gann, not Fibonacci.

Gann discovered a unique relationship between time and price that is still considered accurate today. That relationship is apparent across all markets in all time frames; no successful trader should ignore it. The relationship is very simple and actually was initially discovered by Fibonacci, except Fibonacci had no use for this knowledge—he was busy going broke trying to turn lead into gold.

The time/price relationship follows the rule of 72 and 50% ratios. Some of this is also covered in Elliot Wave analysis but I want to make this simple. Any time pundits of Elliot Wave, W. D. Gann, or Fibonacci start talking they complicate this whole retracement issue so dramatically that you would think the sun rotated around the earth just prior to the moon eating it. People need to just relax and focus on the main issues.

Fifty percent retracements are important because they balance the net inequality between the competing net order flows. That's it. Retracements do not predict price action or portend new highs or lows. Retracements are not predictive. They are historical. The reason Gann, Elliot, and Fibonacci are all included in this discussion is because they happened to notice the relationships first—though they didn't necessarily understand what it might be saying. Fibonacci noticed that a mathematical ratio existed in nature. He assumed that lead and gold would also be subject to this natural ratio but, as we know now, this is not true. This ratio is apparent in nature and in the way things grow; it is not apparent in crowd behaviors, and markets are about crowd behaviors.

Gann asked the question, "What if the market has a ratio and rhythm in and of itself?" Gann thought he had found an answer to that question when he and Elliot noticed that markets appear to have waves that occur with regular frequency and repetition. By combining these two assumptions into a larger assumption, we now have a supposedly "verified" mathematical model to follow in pursuing our trading success.

But the *apparent* relationship is not the same thing as the *real* relationship. The real relationship is what we want to discuss.

Fifty percent retracements happen because once enough buyers square off against enough sellers, only half of those contracts will be profitable. At the 50% number, exactly half the bulls have a profit and half the bears have a profit. When I say this, it is important to note that this is a *net perspective*. The actual result to any one trading account isn't the issue. If you could find a way to look into the total number of open trades, you would see that of the sum total of the open longs, about half of that total number of open contracts will have an open-trade profit—the others will have losses. In other words, if there were 10,000 open longs, around 5,000 of them will have some open-trade gain and the other 5,000 will have some open-trade loss. The exact same situation will be accurate for the shorts. The market is now temporarily balanced from the *net perspective*.

This situation won't last long; it will only take a short time for new buying or selling pressure to come in. Whoever has the *net advantage* at that point will tip the balance. Most of the time it is in the original direction back toward the previous high or low because from the net perspective the late loser entered from the short-term trend—that is, the few days or so just before the 50% level is reached.

This is a factor of the rule of 72. Most market participants operate on a time frame of 72 hours or less. That means that in all the various ways of creating a market timing signal that *now is the time to initiate a position,* most traders have gotten at least one signal in a 72-hour period and have executed, creating net order-flow. Once they have initiated, they must liquidate to accept their open-trade profit or loss. Most methodologies will have given the exit signal within that time frame as well, with the net result that almost everybody has gotten in and out at least once within a 72-hour period. If this process happens at a 50% balance point, the net result is usually a resumption of he previous trend. See Figure 25.1.

HOW TO USE THE RULE

First you must select a significant high or low price previous to the price the market is currently retreating from. When I say *significant price* I mean a price that is around 72 bars back in time; also they are usually weekly, monthly, or daily price points. If we use a bullish scenario, you are looking for a previous important low price *and* the market is retreating from the most recent high. If you use a daily chart, as used in Figure 25.1, your previous low price must be about 72 days/bars back or so, I find that on longer time frames anything substantially less is not as accurate, and anything significantly more is usually ignored by traders as "old data."

Place a 50% retracement study between the old low and the new

FIGURE 25.1 Buying and Selling 50% Retracements—Cash Euro/USD. FOREX, April 2005 to April 2006.

high—that would be your best buy point. That point will be some time in the future that approximately reflects the 72-bar ratio. This is why a price could trade to a high and Gann would say, "By this time next week, the market will trade at _____ (price)." He would be merely projecting his ratios and computations *forward* some amount of that ratio as a price/time relationship. Of course, the opposite would be a sell point if you were tracking a rally in a bear market. But the underlying psychology behind the 50% retracement is not about resumption of a previous trend or a failed reversal; it is about the *late trader who entered in the last 72 hours.*

Most people who initiate a position—about 80% of the total warm bodies sitting in front of a trading screen—are going to do at least one full round turn in the market just prior to the market reaching the 50% price area. The vast majority of those traders are looking to make money *right now*. If they follow standard technical analysis or use any of the most common methodologies, because the market was trending lower for more than 30 bars from the rejected high to the 50% point, they are looking to sell into the market and join the apparent downtrend currently in progress, from their point of view. Their focus is to get positioned on the short side because "the trend is your friend."

But the market has just become balanced momentarily. That means only one thing. The shorts from above the market will cover; they have the most recent 72-hour open-trade profit. The late shorts cover, adding to the buy order imbalance as they take their loss. Last, the old longs on the greater-than-72-bar time frame (the 20% of long-term traders, the ones who know how to follow this rule—*the professionals who know you need more than 72 hours to beat the loser*) add to net winning open positions, many of which they have owned since the turn under the market. They know that the retracement is coming and it will draw in late blood. So they gladly sit through the 50% retracement with at least part of their original position. Of course, the exact opposite scenario develops when a declining market rallies 50%.

Now obviously, markets don't always turn on a dime once they retrace 50%. Sometimes they take more time to balance temporarily; sometimes they need several more or fewer bars than 72; sometimes they sit at the 50% level for a bit and then retrace farther before moving back in the original trend. None of that is the point. The point is, if you want to make a lot of winning trades and keep it simple, enter your position at the 50 percent retracement point and wait. More often than not you will get at least something you can work with.

When you combine this rule with Rules #11, #14, #16, and #17, you have a huge potential to take a lot of money when a market still has more to go and you are willing to wait for it. In fact, you only need a handful of trades a year if you are willing to think ahead more than 72 bars when you are developing a trade hypothesis. Traders who have hit the home run, traders who have been long a bull market when an honest-to-goodness shortage is developing or short an hysterical bull market when the hedgers finally cap the rally, will tell you that when the 50% retracement happened, it was truly a thing of beauty and the money rolled in.

One last thing before we close out this rule: In fairness to all the people out there who are legitimate experts on the theories of Gann, Elliot, and Fibonacci (which I am not), I really don't intend to discredit anyone or their theories. I just think that the essential part of what these men can teach us is best found when we use some simple common sense. No one has a secret method, and there is no perfect technical approach. These great men of history and of the markets found pieces of the deeper truth and expressed it the best they could. Only they could know how to use the sum total of their knowledge in today's markets; the rest is conjecture and opinion by people who never knew them personally.

I think it is important to remember that the essential part of market knowledge is simplicity. Remember, Livermore was a contemporary of Gann and Elliot and made more winnings then they did combined. Livermore never used these kinds of analysis. He understood people and how they behave, so well that he could read a market better than others could analyze a market. I think the best traders are those who read the markets first; I don't think the analysts are thinking along the same lines. Studying Gann, Elliot, or Fibonacci by reading their books is similar to saying you understand Beethoven well because you can read his music scores.

The Only Indicator You Need

You should try to buy weakness and sell strength.
That's the crowd panicking. The problem is, how
do you know they are getting in or getting out?
—Mark Twain, *Discussions with Nikola Tesla*

Many people are unaware that Samuel Clemens (Mark Twain) was a trader. During his time, traders were referred to as "Speculators" and they had a somewhat unsavory reputation. Speculators were seen as exploiters, making money from other people's suffering or need. The worst form of speculator was the carpetbagger who helped rebuild the South with Northern money after the U.S. Civil War. Clemens himself traded in cotton and grains but with little success, according to some biographies of his life.

At the time, the development of futures contracts was in its infancy. The Chicago Board of Trade was only founded in 1848 and probably wouldn't have survived if futures contracts hadn't caught the eye of the visionary industrialists and large farmers. Most of the attention that was focused on market opportunities revolved around the Industrial Revolution somehow. Speculators were often involved in buying land that they hoped to sell to the railroads or lease for the right of way, buying steel to sell to ship builders, and so on. Only occasionally did speculators trade in futures for consumable commodities; it was still a new concept. But even then, during the late 19th century, people saw ahead to the explosive potential in financial markets, and a new class of finance evolved. In today's world, financial brokers are the gateway between market opportunities and capital—even now when electronic trading typically bypasses the traditional brokerage relationship.

One thing that remains constant in the process of financial evolution is the concept of *inside information*. To this day, part of what people view as a *trading edge* is knowing something ahead of time that is potentially market moving. This is not quite the same thing as a tip. Getting a tip means being advised what to do by someone who allegedly knows something. Market information or trading edge is more about finding a better way to do something that is already known to work. In the opening quote for this rule, it is apparent that Clemens understood the basic nature of the market and knew it could be exploited; his problem was getting the information required to know whether he was in the right place at the right time. This is where the whole business of analysis and indicators came from—an attempt to quantify market information to exploit what already works. The basics of trading have never really changed.

Remember, some of the biggest fortunes ever made from trading came at a time when the only tools available to traders were their guts, intuition, and knowledge of the crowd. I say this because, as you will have guessed by now, I put only a small part of my trade study into technical analysis. I know many will stop there and form some sort of value judgment. They might assume that because I don't use what they have used, and they are making money with it, I must not know what they know; perhaps I don't know the experts they know, or maybe I just have an axe to grind. They might say I am not qualified to discuss technical analysis because I don't use technical analysis the way they do. The proof is in the pudding, they would argue.

I say this about big-money traders and historical finance because success *without* analysis is factual history—not because I feel that analysis has no place in trading. Quite the opposite. Successful technical analysis can be a very important part of lasting trading success but, as discussed in Rule #15, like it or not, it can only go so far. The fact is that using technical analysis is like an unskilled carpenter using power tools. Without the basic knowledge of carpentry, an unskilled carpenter will make a wreck of house building when he is turned loose with better tools than he knows how to use. That brings us to this maxim of "the only indicator you need."

But first we should clarify the thinking behind most of the indicators currently used. Most indicators and oscillators attempt to quantify the concept of *overbought* or *oversold*. The psychology behind this thinking is actually very sound, in my opinion. The idea that the market can get overextended in one direction or the other is not a new idea. It is one of the cornerstones of successful trading. That is one of the concepts that will work for successful traders. The problem is not that the market can and will get overextended; the difficulty is in calculating when that point is reached. Oscillators and indicators are notorious for being *lagging* indicators for the simple fact that they are *historical* and not *predictive*. In most cases, due to the historical nature of these calculated mathematical concepts, they have often identified a reasonable overbought or oversold area but by the time the signal is verified, the 72-hour/bar rule (from Rule #25) has come into play. The market you suspected was overextended has already begun correcting the other way, and usually that distance has been a substantial move already. Also, most oscillators and indicators are trend *following*; they help you get positioned in a trend but will never get you positioned at the turn. In addition, by the time the signal to enter the trend is verified and you execute, the very next correction will likely be right back to your entry price or a bit lower. No real progress in any case.

The newest class of oscillators and indicators attempt to be *predictive* in nature. Many of them are based on extremely complex computations that can only be done in real time by computers. We call traders who use them the "black box" traders. Again, there is nothing wrong with this kind of approach except that it simply cannot account for the most critical part of trading: *What is the crowd thinking?*

It is crucial to remember when you are using oscillators or indicators of any kind that they are only mathematical computations. They are all moving averages in various degrees of complexity and performance. They are based on assumptions about the nature of markets and they work under the theory of probabilities. Behind all of these attempts to find a better way to do what is already known to work is the issue of *historical* versus *predictive*. If you are willing to accept that indicators, oscillators, and technical analysis are historical and not predictive, you are left with the only indicator you really need: Who is getting in and who is getting out?

That brings us to the study of volume and open interest. In my view, this is the only indicator you really need because this is the only indicator that discloses fairly accurately what the crowd is thinking. Either people are getting into the market or they are leaving the market. Since we already know that most active traders are losing every day, then we know that a change in open interest means people don't want to play, are convinced they will win, or can't take the pain any more. If open interest rises we can fairly safely assume that traders are confident to get into the market from both sides. If open interest is dropping we can safely assume the losers can't take the heat anymore. If all of this is accompanied by higher or lower volume, then we can fairly safely judge the level of fear, panic, or hope that traders are expressing.

Now, to be fair with everyone, correctly reading volume and open interest is not as simple as I make it sound. But the underlying psychology will always be the same. By understanding the relationship between price action, volume, and open interest, you can get a fairly accurate read on what the crowd is thinking. Of course, this is an art form and not science. Markets can change in character in a heartbeat and your understanding of V/OI may have been completely accurate 20 minutes ago but at this precise moment *something has changed*. That is the dynamic part of trading and part of what makes V/OI so useful. V/OI is the first indicator developed, and everything after is an attempt to improve upon what V/OI can do with one important difference: *V/OI has no time/price relationship*.

V/OI is historical from the point of view that it discloses how *big* the market is or whether that has changed somewhat. V/OI also discloses how *thick* the market is and whether that, too, is changing. When you combine this information with a price advance or decline, you can discern whether more shorts or longs are opening positions or covering, whether they are executing more often or not, whether they are losing confidence in their positions, and a host of other types of information that make it possible to *anticipate* (not predict!) what is most likely to happen next. Once the market closes for the day and this data is compiled and released by the exchanges, you have a fairly accurate picture of the mind of the market when you compare what you see to the price action and other indicators.

But because V/OI has no time/price component, you may see clearly that the market is setting up for a price advance or decline but there is no way to know how soon or how fast that change in price will occur. Although V/OI is the single most important indicator because it discloses the most likely thought process behind how prices got to be where they are, it still cannot predict or expose whether that thought process is ripe for change or whether the change is imminent. That is the whole purpose of all the so-called improved indicators and oscillators: to find the time/price relationship for that imminent change. The V/OI indicator shows you it is there; the others try to say the time is now.

If you personally had to choose between the two indications, "Something in the market has changed" and "Whatever is coming, it will come at 11:00 A.M. tomorrow," which would you rather have? In the case of the markets, knowing that something has changed is the better choice because only one option is available: a reversal in price. Does it really matter if that reversal happens in the coming 20 minutes or if it will take 20 days, as long as you know that the change will most likely be in only the other direction?

As I have said many times before, I am not trying to oversimplify the issue of timing your trades. My intention is to help you understand that the first and best indicator will always be volume and open interest because it provides a more critical component: the issue of *a change to the structure of the market*. In most cases, a change to the structure of the market means a price reversal of some kind because the traders who put the price where it is are no longer in the market. The thinking of the crowd has changed. Just knowing that piece of information can give your trading a distinct advantage. You just don't know precisely when the change will result in a price reversal.

Before we close out this rule I want to sum up a few things. First, the study of V/OI is not a small one. You need to make a consistent effort to understand how V/OI can and does change. It would be impossible in this book to have a discussion about all the different ways you can begin to interpret V/OI in the space we have. I have included titles in the Recommended Reading section that will help you better understand this important market study. Second, you must remember that all the other indicators and oscillators developed in the past 150 years are attempts to better quantify the *price/time relationship* with V/OI as the foundation to start from. V/OI quantifies the depth and nature of the game as it has been played to date; V/OI tells you a change has happened or is happening. What you do with that data is a reflection of your skill at anticipating what is likely to happen next based on your understanding of the crowd's needs.

Last, V/OI is never predictive. No indicator or oscillator can be predictive. No form of analysis can predict future price action with any degree of consistency. The important issue is to have the tools you need, and to know how to use them to improve upon what *already works*.

Samuel Clemens and the traders of his era didn't have V/OI or any other indicator. If he did, he would have known exactly how to use it and what it means because he understood the basics to begin with. Focus your energy on learning the basics, then understanding V/OI. At that point the rest of your trading stands a good chance of falling into place as a winning approach.

Study Winning Traders

We should accustom the mind to keep the best company by introducing it only to the best books.
—Sydney Smith, *Forbes Thoughts on Opportunity*

Most people would agree that learning to do anything well involves many things working together in harmony. Various parts of the educational process carry different weight with each individual, and in today's world we suffer from information overload. Education as a *process* needs to be prioritized for each person differently because each individual may begin from a unique starting point. Reducing information overload is a critical part of the process, I feel, because with the Internet now in full swing, we can literally see everything ever discussed on any topic, if we have the time or the interest. Trading is no different. There is a voluminous amount of data available at the click of a mouse, most of which won't help you succeed, in my view. You need to know how to prioritize what you evaluate.

Narrowing your focus to get the best trade education can be done a lot better by taking a step back and asking yourself a few questions. The best one is: Who specifically should I listen to? The answer is that there really are only two people you absolutely need to be listening to. The first is you. In Rule #10 we discussed record keeping as part of the process of educating ourselves to become better traders. By documenting our behavior we gain insight into our thinking. We can get the same benefit from other people's documentation if we choose. In addition to Rule #28, "Be a student of yourself," I think it is equally important to learn what has worked for other successful traders. No one in this business has a mortgage on the truth, and anyone who is a consistent net winning trader has something valuable to say. That information is contained in the books they write or the books that have been written about them. So the only person besides yourself you should listen to is every other successful trader. Between these two people you will eventually get 100% of what you need to develop and maintain a winning approach.

Now, when I say "Listen to other successful traders," I don't mean "Listen to people who have a product to sell." That may not be a good thing for the limited resources most people have when they begin trading. One of the more confusing parts of developing a winning trade approach is that there is a lot of market-related information out there to look at. Between the books, magazines, trading systems, audio series, seminars, free data, and so on, you could spend all kinds of money and waste all kinds of time and never get any farther along than you are now. In fact, I am part of that process. I personally offer a live six-week seminar designed to improve your market presence, and one of the objections I always get from potential attendees is, "How is this course going to help me trade?" Rather than take time here for those kinds of arguments or issues, let me just say that you have to weed through a lot of poor-quality information to get to the things that will help you. Personally, I don't teach people to trade. I teach them to think for themselves.

The point is that you as a trader can shorten your learning curve by education, but you need to be careful how you approach the educational process. You run the risk of investing a large amount of your personal resources into places that will not help you advance your trading career. In order to prevent that from happening, I want to offer you a few suggestions about how to narrow your focus and get truly high-quality market education for the money you have to invest in that direction.

Be sensitive and focus on the difference between *trading systems* and *trading*. Trading systems are methodologies for improving trade *selection*—in other words, ways to find a better place to go long or short. These trading systems are based on probabilities and past market performance, and they are often designed by people with little *trading* experience. Often trading systems are computer software programs you can buy or try for free, books that describe the method and illustrate it with past markets, or even multiple-day seminars taught by the developer of the system directly. This is learning a trading *system*, not *trading*.

Trading is the far more critical element and needs to be the central issue in your education. Many very good trading systems are worthless to most users of that system because the real issues of trading are never addressed. Learning to trade involves learning how to avoid common mistakes, control your behavior, avoid emotional interference, and effectively manage risk. A great *trading system* will not work if the user keeps second-guessing the trade signals, doubling up on trades that are losing, scaring himself out of a winner too soon, or making a host of other missteps. Simply stated, a winning trading system is completely negated by poor trading.

All successful traders learned how to avoid bad behavior while developing or using a system. The surprising thing they all will tell the developing trader is that the trading system is the smallest part of their approach. Every winning trader uses a slightly different approach, and they cover the gamut of potential behaviors. Some winning traders are day traders, some scalpers, some position or swing traders, some spread traders; the list is endless. Trading systems can vary, but trading cannot.

In my opinion, the best use of your educational capital is to divide your education into both parts but spend more time on learning *trading*. Personally, I invest a few hundred dollars each year on books, tapes, and seminars. Since I don't need to learn a system methodology anymore, I buy resources that are biographical in nature. I study winning *traders*, not trading systems. Every year I go hear winning traders speak, read books they have written, or listen to audios they have recorded. By far the greatest return on investment has been focusing on *how winners think* rather than *how winners trade*. Because trading is a subjective and personal experience, it is unreasonable to think that some other trader's approach will be compatible with my own or with my trading nature. It is far more plausible to expect that winning behaviors are learned from experience, and that by seeing someone else's experience as similar to my own, I could learn how to improve my own behavior or avoid developing bad behavior. Most winning traders will tell you they had a combination-type experience of their own. They had to find or develop a trading system compatible with their personality or nature, but the biggest thing for them was learning to effectively *trade*.

The best way to communicate this difference and why it is so important is to draw an illustration from something that really counts. Imagine you are a soldier sent to the front of the action. Regardless of what you would like to believe about the nature of this particular military conflict, the fact is someone on the other side of the battlefield is trying to kill you. It is not a video game or a training exercise. This time you are under real threat for your life. You don't have a choice at this point, and certainly you are not the person to negotiate a peaceful resolution to the conflict; at this particular moment it is a question of kill or be killed. Your enemy is faced with the exact same situation, and you can rest assured that he is thinking the same thing about you. You don't want to die and neither does he. By the end of the day this situation will change and one of you will be dead.

Up walks the commanding officer and he gives you an order. He orders you and your squad of soldiers out into the heart of the conflict to establish a forward position for the coming offensive. You turn around and see that your commanding officer is a 23-year-old first lieutenant, just graduated from West Point Military Academy. He is assuming his first command after graduation and his orders are, "Go establish a forward position." You are being ordered into combat by someone with little or no combat experience, and if he makes a mistake you run the risk of going home in a body bag right then and there.

Obviously, a trained soldier would execute that order, and I am not suggesting that new military officers are not qualified. I am illustrating the point that, like it or not, book knowledge is different from combat experience. Our hypothetical soldier would feel a lot less conflict about establishing a forward position if the commanding officer was a three-star general who has fought for his life many times and has personally beaten this particular enemy army twice before. That general will most likely not order a soldier into a losing position. At one point, that three-star general was a first lieutenant newly graduated from West Point as well, along with a group of other potential combat officers that year. They are all dead and he is not. He learned how to apply the book knowledge better under combat and that is why he is a three-star general. Most likely he will see the traps and pitfalls the enemy might try to set, and because he has beaten this enemy more than once he knows how to exploit the weakness the enemy can't see.

Trading is a lot like that. It really is a kill-or-be-killed environment. All the book knowledge you have will not help when you are on the wrong side of the net order flow; you are losing the war at that point. Only combat experience will help you. Net winning traders have developed winning behaviors from being in the heat of the battle and not getting themselves killed. You as a developing trader will learn more from studying winning traders than you will from studying theory, just like winning military officers learn more from combat than they do from books.

The list of Recommended Reading at the end of this book includes titles I found very helpful for the study of winning traders. All of the books are readily available, and if you read them all you will most likely learn more. I would encourage you to continue making the study of winning traders a regular part of your trading approach. I am not suggesting that you ignore new developments in the art and science of market analysis. In my view, I think you will come to the same conclusion that I have. After enough time most of the market study you explore is all saying pretty much the same thing. By balancing your education between trading systems and trading, you will shorten your learning curve, without going around in circles while you trade your way to zero equity.

To make this rule work for you, your best bet is to discipline yourself to spend enough time daily to read one chapter of a good trader biography daily. Within one year you will have read several biographies of people who have won the war more than once. You will leverage their experience into your own.

Be a Student of Yourself

In the land of the blind, the one-eyed man is king.
—Old Yiddish saying

I think the hardest thing for most people to develop is a truly transparent point of view about themselves. All of us have strengths and weaknesses. We all have degrees of misconceptions about ourselves and the world around us. We have character flaws and unique talents. We have all made mistakes and we have all had successes. No matter how you slice it, every human being is an individual first before being part of a group. That individuality is expressed differently by each person. The sum total of those individualities becomes our circle of influence, our friends and neighbors, our towns and governments, and ultimately part of the total human experience—the history we participate in.

Within that moment-to-moment expression of our individuality as it becomes our history, there is the corresponding potential that some of us (as individuals) will choose to express the negative, dark side of our potentials. The individual who refuses to accept the responsibility to behave reasonably becomes the criminal we have to incarcerate; the circle of friends who all think in that criminal way becomes the street gang we have to be protected from; the government more interested in itself than in its people becomes the rogue nation that threatens everyone; and so on.

Each of our individual expressions, for better or worse, becomes the never-ending cycle of group behavior, which in turn becomes economic good times and bad, the daily pleasures and pains we have in life, laws we

167

have to follow, the times of war and peace—and, believe it or not: the cycle of bulls and bears. When the individuals form into a group, the group is at the mercy of the prevailing total of the individuals' input. The marketplace is unique because even though the market is a group and subject to group behavior, each individual can participate at any time he or she chooses, while the total group goes on with or without that individual. Our individual participation helps create the group and we can exploit the group, but that is also an individual choice too.

In my opinion, the single biggest problem facing each of us as traders is knowing where to draw the line in our individual thinking as it then becomes our individual actions imposed on the group. We need to understand what creates our urge to action. Every one of us has a unique expression of how we handle data input and what that means. For some of us, a sharp rally in a market stimulates our desire for a profit by focusing on the market getting "too high"; we might be looking for a short. Other traders will see that as a breakout and will jump on the market from the buy side. Some will do nothing and wait for a pullback to buy, or see a pullback as a confirmation of a failed high before selling.

In all cases, the price action is simply there; it just is. All of those various ways of making a conclusion are unique to the individual. They come from inside of us and are solely determined by how we personally choose to see things. Every trader participating in every market is choosing to see things a certain way; they are all unique individuals using the markets as a form of expression for this conclusion-making process. We all execute our trades from a unique point of view. But in all cases, the price action itself is the same for everybody. We as individuals form the conclusion as to what it means. The group itself is impervious to this. The group just goes on, with or without us.

In your trader development you will sooner or later be faced with a losing trade that makes no sense to you. This is a factor of how you attached meaning to the price action that created your urge to action, your participation. The group had nothing to do with that evaluation and conclusion-making process. Once you join the group in progress, you are at the mercy of the group's behavior as a sum total of every other trader's individual participation, too. If the trade you selected is a loser, that loser had nothing to do with how you came to the conclusion that it was time to participate; it is a factor of everyone else's participation. Your choice came from inside you; your results came from inside the group.

It is for this reason that your personal, unique individual expression of your conclusion-making process needs to become as transparent to you as you can make it. Unless your conclusion is of the sort that the group potential is in your favor, you have little or no chance for a gain once you execute and place yourself at risk. This transparency is something that is not a natural state for most people, for the simple reason that our daily lives do not require it. You can go through life never once working on your character imperfections or your weaknesses and still have a very nice life, for all intents and purposes. It is usually only when our weaknesses or flaws become glaringly obvious that we are willing to address them, such as an addiction problem. The world is full of horrible people who get on just fine no matter how much destruction they create around them. The world is also full of wonderful people who get on just fine. Once we all decide to trade in the same markets, and create a group none of us has control over, everything changes. The biggest idiot in the group can profit if he is on the right side of the net order flow, and the Nobel Prize winner will have a loss if he is on the wrong side. It's as simple as that.

So why do we need to study ourselves? Because when we understand *why* we do what we do the way we do, we are no longer at the mercy of the group. Until our thinking and behavior is divorced from the group's thinking and behavior, we cannot see the group's thinking or behavior for what it really is. The crowd or group is behaving from its conclusion-making structure. That structure is called the *herd*. Until we can see clearly how a herd functions, we cannot know when to get out of the way of the herd or steer the herd.

We must rise above the average thinking process coming from an unregenerate mind. We must study our own thinking and behavior to recognize when it is destructive or profitable. When we see the herd choosing to behave destructively we have the opportunity to behave profitably. Because the market is a crowd, a group, and a herd, it will *never* function from anything except the sum total of the individuals' behavior—and that is *always* at the lower end of the spectrum as long as the group is made of people who can't see they are destructive. Most traders have net losses because they think and behave very similarly to every other member of the group. When a trader chooses to think and behave differently, he is the only one available for new information about the structure of the group. This difference comes from self-analyzing your thinking and dissecting your behavior until you see clearly how you are performing exactly like the crowd or in some other unique manner. Once you know this difference, and it doesn't have to be by a wide margin, you will finally buy weakness and sell strength often enough to win.

It is easy to say "Be a student of yourself," but what are the practical aspects of making a commitment to develop this skill of transparency?

No matter your personal state of development, you have to come to the understanding that this process of developing transparency is about lifting the veil of illusion. The price of knowledge is the destruction of illusion. People who will not let go of their illusions are the ones who suffer the most. In the trading arena the illusions we operate under come to full confrontation very quickly. Some traders call this process *forced awareness*. By this they mean that your personal conclusion-making process is what it is and when you have losses in your account you are *wrong*. If a trader excuses his loss in any manner, he is operating under illusion until his money is all gone. Now the trader has only one choice: Admit that he has an illusion problem or deny it further. If the trader is truly on the pathway to transparency, the total loss in his account came from forced awareness. The trader cannot deny that the results in his account are *because of his actions alone*. This is why self-study leading to self-awareness is so important. Without it you will experience forced awareness. Which do you prefer?

To avoid experiencing forced awareness, you can start the process of confronting your personal depth of illusion anytime. Most people do not like what they see about themselves when they do, or will not accept they really have that particular issue. This is why an *intervention* can be so effective when confronting people with addiction problems, because until that point, the addict really doesn't think he has a problem. When confronted with a choice between the drug and the friendship, the die is cast. The responsibility is now with the addict. In trading, you must be both the problem and the solution. You have to confront yourself or the market will do it for you. It is a choice—keep the illusion or keep your money. Which do you want most?

To consistently confront myself, so that I reduce the amount of illusion I might be operating under, I have a stack of note cards with questions written on them. I ask myself every day, "Am I hoping the market will go my way?" "Am I afraid to execute?" "Am I trusting something besides myself to earn a profit today?" or numerous other questions. I also have note cards with reminders on them such as "Wait for the market to hit the stops before executing," "The market does not know my position," "Follow your rules 100%," and others as well. The point is that for me personally I have found that my tendency to illusion is lessened if I remind myself daily what the basics are and what the rules are. I no longer have the conversations with myself or others that involve opinion about price action, what the fundamentals will do to prices, what some talking head in the press has to say, and so on. I no longer think like the crowd, so I now know how to exploit that crowd thinking.

I have to do this daily because I also know I have a tendency to overconfidence. When I am winning consistently I am tempted to think I know what I am doing. That is an illusion as well, and right about then I start losing. Since I am tired of losing and don't want to do it any more, I am willing to do whatever it takes to remain a winner, even if that means my pet illusions about myself end up in the trash can.

Please understand, in this short description of this rule it is impossible to give you a detailed pathway for developing transparency and avoiding forced awareness. Again, the Recommended Reading section includes titles that will provide you with great places to start this process of changing your thinking enough to exploit the crowd. But there is no easy way. Always remember that every trader had to learn to trade. No one at the top of his or her game got there by accident, and all successful traders will tell you that the first blowout taught them not to rely on illusion. It started them on the pathway to true understanding.

That understanding is that the market is created inside your own head. How you see things determines how you will trade. Learn to see things in a new way. All the other rules are designed to keep you in the game until you can see clearly how to out-think the crowd.

Conclusion

Remember, the market doesn't beat a player. It merely gives him the chance to beat himself.
—The 1989 Commodity Trader's Almanac

I really enjoyed writing this book. As I said in the Introduction, I took time to answer questions I hadn't thought of before. In looking at things from a fresh perspective and attempting to write concisely, I rediscovered old truths in a new way while becoming reacquainted with the basics more completely. I sincerely hope you have enjoyed reading and that you have acquired at least one new concept you can apply to improve your approach. I know I have. But seeing as this is for you, let me offer you a conclusion.

Trading is not what people think it is. It is tempting to believe that successful speculation is a factor of economic fundamentals, political influences, supply and demand, being in the right place at the right time, and a little foresight, all rolled into one. We can convince ourselves that with enough study and enough knowledge, combined with enough perseverance and some critical timing, we will find our fortune waiting on the other side of our hard work like a pot of gold at the end of the rainbow. But the truth of trading is more like the sirens calling over the waves, wooing us to a certain shipwreck if we aren't careful.

As you put together your trading approach and look for your edge, I think this whole book can be summed up with the understanding that your success is not *outside of you*. Your success is *inside of you*. If you have been reading between the lines, you probably have come to the conclusion that *every* trading rule is related to every other rule on some level. All of these rules that work have an underlying psychology that includes nonattachment to results, the recognition that anything can happen, and the understanding that the crowd doesn't know what it is doing. Since we operate from a certain point of reference in order to create opportunities from the apparent randomness of price action, all we really need to do is remain vigilant enough to get out when we are losing and stay in when we are winning. The less energy we put into forming value judgments about prices, expecting the market to do one thing over another, or trying to fix what isn't broken, and the faster we will admit we are wrong, the more potential for net gains we will have. When you think about the underlying psychology of that kind of behavior you come to the inescapable conclusion that we control our destiny as traders with more certainty than we control the rest of our lives. When we realize that, our potential trading will truly be effortless and without inner conflict.

I think that most traders will admit that up to a certain point, or even currently, their trading has been frustrating, painful, irritating, or filled with some other negative emotional conflict. All of what we surround ourselves with as part of our daily trading routine are often designed to help minimize or eliminate this inner conflict. But almost all of what we feel as inner conflict has nothing to do with the market. We create that conflict from how we choose to view what is happening or from internalizing what it all means for our trading balance. The market is just a machine processing orders. How can a machine create so much conflict in our daily lives?

The machine has nothing to do with the conflict. Stop and think about how silly it is to get angry with your car if you run out of gas. The car told you *very clearly* it needed gas with that little flashing light next to the "E" on the gas gauge. You created the conflict by ignoring the very clear signals the car itself was giving you. You don't have to experience the conflict; just stop and get gas. If that means you will be late for a date, then your problem is time management; that is not the car's fault. For some people, trading is like driving with a broken gas gauge down a deserted country road between towns. They have no idea when the car will quit, so every mile is a sense of impending doom. In trading, the problem is not with the market (the machine) but in our failure to manage ourselves.

The point of *Trading Rules that Work* is to free your mind from the consequences of your emotional state. If you are still developing your trade approach, controls on your behavior will prevent you from executing bad trading behavior. Bad behavior will surely result in losses, and if those losses are complicated by severe negative emotions, your mental energy is taken up with trying to eliminate pain instead of finding opportunity. That is exactly how the crowd is thinking; that is why so many traders have net losses when they don't have to. Can you imagine a road full of people tearing their hair out, yelling at their out-of-gas cars, when there is a gas station at every intersection as far as the eye can see?

Traders tend to complicate things needlessly when they add emotional pressure on top of basic pressures. Losses in the market are a fact of life, and many are avoidable. But when you beat yourself up for the loss and wonder ceaselessly if the loss could have been avoided, you add stress to a process that is stressful enough without your help. There is no need for that. Take a step back and *think*.

To develop your full trading potential you need a different paradigm of thought. This doesn't mean you have to change your entire world and life view (although that helped me). All you really need to do is ask yourself really good questions and have the courage to answer those questions honestly, without kidding or deluding yourself. All of the rules discussed in this book are places to connect with that new paradigm. While you are altering your point of view to be more in line with the scope of market/crowd thinking and behavior, the controls on your behavior prevent you from giving away all your capital. Change is not something that happens overnight anyway, so I think it is unreasonable for any trader to think he will make money without some basic education. The rules you create and impose for yourself are like having a set time to go to class every day. You won't get educated without going to class, and you have to be at class on time. You won't make money trading until you learn what you need to know, and the rules insure you will be in class. Once you have your education, you don't have to go to class. Once you know how to trade, you can change and improve your rules if you choose to keep them.

Regardless of how you want to look at it, the problem and the solution lies within you—not the market. Try to remain the sort of trader who fully accepts responsibility for his results. Remember that you choose to execute. No matter what you use to gain enough confidence to pull the trigger, you and you alone make that choice. Your analysis, fear, greed, hope, and lack of knowledge are all parts of that decision-making process until you reach the point of full control of your actions. Having controls on your behavior puts you in a place where your inner confidence can grow while you develop better outer behavior. As you see that your behavior can be consistent and profitable, you gain confidence in what will work for you. You learn to execute better, you accept your results no matter what they are, you discover your trading strengths, and your trading weaknesses are addressed in a way that you can accept. Once you fully accept your responsibility and fully control your actions, trading becomes effortless and pleasurable instead of frustrating and painful.

But all of that change happened inside you. The market is just the market and would have been there with or without you while those changes were made. So in the final analysis, you created your opportunity—not the markets.

Before we close I want to give you a few particulars that will help you develop your personal rules from these 28 guidelines. First, your rules have to be personal. They need to be from inside you. I suggest you use a lot of "I," "me," and "my" in your rules. For example, don't make the rule "Only risk 30 points on a trade." Make the rule: "I only risk 30 points on my initial trade." When you personalize your rules they have a greater impact on your thinking. The rules are no longer just good ideas floating around out there; they are personal behaviors you do every day.

I also suggest that you write them inside quotation marks to make them your words when you read them, and read them out loud so you can hear them in your own voice. Have you ever had the experience when you were about to do something and you heard your mother's voice inside your head telling you not to do that? Whether or not you did the behavior isn't the point. I bet for certain you stopped and thought about it before you did or did not do it.

Second, review your rules at least twice a day. I read my rules in the morning before I get to my desk and after I do my daily market study at the end of the day. I am in the habit of opening my trading day and closing my trading day with a review of my rules. Psychological studies have shown that if you begin and end the day with a consistent positive reinforcement you sleep better, and you also perform better the next day. That is probably why kids always want to be tucked into bed at night. They seem to have no problem getting up early . . .

Also, make a consistent time away from the trading desk to do your market analysis. I find that when I am not staring at a computer screen I am not tempted to reevaluate my trading in real-time. Following Rule #14 is much easier if you are sitting somewhere away from the market doing your analysis with a paper printout and a calculator. At the end of the day, I print out my charts and any relevant information or studies and lock myself in one of the unused cubicles in my office. I find that when I am away from the actual price action and totally alone without distraction, I can focus a lot better. Often I have remembered something or made a decision about something that I would have missed if I was in the heat of battle.

Last, next to all the rules in Part II, I think Rule #21 is the most important rule to follow as a new trader while you are developing your approach. Once you have settled on a risk-control strategy to cut losses, the next thing is to block out everything and *think on your own*. Of course, you need market research and commentary, but it is the *way you use it* that will make all the difference. Rather than accept at face value what you read and hear, ask good questions about what traders would be tempted to do with that data. Sooner or later all market data creates an urge to action, which results in a trade creating pressure on the order flow. Ask yourself, "What have traders done already with this data?" or "What will other traders think this means?" When people around you offer market commentary, politely excuse yourself or tell them outright to shut up. The single best way to get a tipster to stay away is to ask him to show you his account balance. In my opinion, nothing will slow you down faster than failing to follow Rule #21.

Other than these few thoughts, the floor is open. Every reader will have a different way of enforcing these 28 guidelines. I would love to hear how you personally have been able to apply what you are learning. Feel free to drop me a line in care of Wiley; they will see that I get it. Also, readers are welcome to join me for my regular daily Internet broadcasts. Details are at my web site, www.proedgefx.com. Thanks for reading.

Recommended Reading

There is no end to the discussion of things. Endless devotion to books and the study of opinion is tiresome and wearying to the mind.
—King Solomon, Ecclesiastes 12:12

I have read hundreds of books relating to the markets, trading, and psychology. At one time my library of related material was larger than most people's total libraries combined. I also had piles of newspapers, trade magazines, audio/videotape series, and general notes from seminars I attended. Once I reached a certain point in my education as a trader, I decided that most of it was all saying the same basic thing with usually one or two fine points that really mattered. I took the point of view that whatever I had spent in dollars was an investment into my trading skill, and as long as I learned one thing that helped me add one more winning trade or prevent one more losing trade, this was all money well spent.

After a certain point I found myself focusing on a few books that I felt were the important ones. That is not to say that the other data I had collected wasn't useful. It's just that there is virtually an unlimited amount of data you could expose yourself to if you wanted to, especially with the available Internet resources, not to mention the huge investment you could make of both time and money. At some point you need to narrow your focus—otherwise you could find yourself spending more time studying than trading, and more money on education rather than trade capital.

I felt it was time to clean house. I threw out or gave away huge amounts of market-related data but decided to keep what I felt were the essential needed things. I now have a much smaller library and also don't buy as much new stuff. As I wrote in Rule #27, I still invest a certain amount of time and money in continuing education, but it is a lot less and more focused now. I think that as a trader you can gain a lot from this point of view because it will help you spend less time and money by not acquiring the same basic information compiled into another format. You can also benefit because your learning curve may be shortened.

The books listed in this section are the ones that I feel cover the essential elements to developing a winning trade approach and creating trading rules that will work for you. I think it is important to reiterate that all the rules you choose to use for yourself are self-created and self-imposed. The reason I feel these books cover the basics well is because they all have a common theme. All of these books start from the premise that the trader himself is the most critical component to lasting success. All of the building blocks discussed that are market related, such as technical indicators and so forth, usually are covered in deep enough detail that very little more can be added to the discussion. Also, most of the psychology discussed as it relates to rule making, trading approaches, money management, and so on, continues to support the point of view that the individual needs to become fully in control of his actions when he trades. We can't control the market; we can only control ourselves.

Some of the books are not market related at all, but I included them because I feel they expose the crowd thinking/behavior connection well. The books are listed in alphabetical order by author—no special endorsement for any one book or author is intended. I include a brief description of why I like each one. And finally, no compensation was given to me to select these books. I genuinely feel the author and the subject are valuable enough to include them in the list.

Abell, Howard, and Robert Koppell. *The Inner Game of Trading*. Chicago: Probus Publishing, 1994. Focuses on the relationship between thought and action. Helps clarify the difference between intents and desires.

Carret, Philip L. *The Art of Speculation*. Burlington, VT: Fraser Publishing Company, 1930. Great book on tactics, several useful methods for effective positioning, lots on equities.

Douglas, Mark. *The Disciplined Trader*. New York: New York Institute of Finance, 1990. Critical discussion of zero-sum psychology. Lots on staying focused on your method.

Douglas, Mark. *Trading in the Zone*. New York: Prentice Hall, 2000. More on the daily discipline to your method, seeing trading as a holistic experience.

Koppel, Robert. *The Tao of Trading*. Chicago: Dearborn Financial Publishing, 1998. Point of view includes focus and understanding regarding consistency. How world and life view affects execution.

Le Bon, Gustave. *The Crowd: A Study of the Popular Mind*. Atlanta: Cherokee Publishing Company, 1895. (Reprinted by Fraser Publishing Co., 1982) Early work on defining the factors that contribute to and disclose crowd behavior.

Lefèvre, Edwin. *Reminiscences of a Stock Operator*. Burlington, VT: Fraser Publishing Company, 1928. (Reprinted by John Wiley & Sons, 2006.) Autobiography of Jesse Livermore. In my view the best all-around work on what makes or breaks the trader. A must-have in any trader's library.

Longstreet, Roy W. *Viewpoints of a Commodity Trader*. Greenville, SC: Trader's Press, 1967. Lots of small one- or two-page thoughts on maintaining a strong market presence. Great for keeping thoughts and emotions balanced.

Mackay, Charles. *Extraordinary Popular Delusions and the Madness of Crowds*. New York: Harmony Books, 1841. (Reprinted by Three Rivers Press, 1995.) Excellent historical documentation of failed beliefs, manias, panics, and eccentric behavior accepted as current scientific truths.

Millman, Gregory J. *The Vandals' Crown*. New York: The Free Press, 1995. History of the rise of FOREX trading. Documents the failure of governments to account for or control currency pricing.

Neill, Humphrey Bancroft. *The Art of Contrary Thinking*. Greenville, NC: Traders Press, 1954. Definitive book on thinking outside the box.

Rogers, Jim. *Hot Commodities*. New York: Random House, 2004. Current megatrends on consumables. Will be out of date someday but still outlines great long-term potential in current markets plus thoughts on how to find great long-term trades.

Schwager, Jack D. *Market Wizards*. New York: New York Institute of Finance, 1987. Interviews with top traders from all markets. Timeless.

Schwager, Jack D. *The New Market Wizards*. New York: HarperCollins, 1992. Updated interviews with more top traders, new focus on trading styles.

Shaleen, Kenneth. *Volume and Open Interest*. Chicago: Probus Publishing, 1991. Critical study on market structure, how crowd behavior can be disclosed by V/OI, effective tools for identifying potential trend changes.

Sperandeo, Victor. *Methods of a Wall Street Master*. Canton, NJ: John Wiley & Sons, 1991. Great all-around work on trader discipline. Trader Vic is completely honest and very well-thought-out discussions are provided.

Tolle, Eckhart. *The Power of Now*. Novato, CA: New World Library, 1997. Tolle's experience with enlightenment. How the Western mind defeats itself (in all endeavors) and what will make a critical difference.

X, Trader. *Dancing With Lions*. Ashland, OH: Bookmasters, 1999. Autobiography—author focuses on detachment and the power of conviction. Detailed discussion on trader evolution, some basic trade methods also.

About the Author

J ason Alan Jankovsky is a full-time trader working from downtown Chicago. He began his career as a Series III Commodities Broker in May 1987 after trading as an independent customer for more than a year prior. During the intervening years he has been involved in almost all facets of the futures industry and also the cash FOREX markets. Currently he works on behalf of public traders as an educator for the customer group of Infinity Brokerage Services and their sister company ProEdgeFX, both headquartered in downtown Chicago. In addition to broadcasting live a twice-daily foreign exchange commentary, he contributes to several regular online publications, is a regular commentator on FOREXTV.com, and teaches the "Psychology of Trading" course for traders around the globe. He is a private pilot and avid sailor.

Details of Mr. Jankovsky's broadcasts can be found at www .proedgefx.com. He can be reached directly at Infinity Brokerage at 1-800-531-2817 or by e-mail at webinar@infinitybrokerage.com.

Index

Page numbers followed by *f* indicate a figure.